THE
SCHOOL
MANAGEMENT
HANDBOOK

THE
SCHOOL
MANAGEMENT
HANDBOOK

Edited by

Jim Donnelly

KOGAN
PAGE

FREE EDUCATIONAL RESOURCES

United Kingdom Nirex Limited has available a range of FREE educational materials, aimed mainly at secondary school level (Key Stage 4), outlining the Company's activities.

This includes:

– a teachers pack for the 14-19 curriculum consisting of a colour folder, teachers notes, project cards and a poster. Each project card contains a combination of informative text and illustrations and a series of tasks for pupils.

– a variety of booklets – with teachers notes where appropriate – some prepared by education publishers.

– videos with accompanying booklets, for example the award winning 'Safe for all Time'.

These FREE educational materials are available on request to:

The Information Office, UK Nirex Ltd., Curie Avenue, Harwell, Didcot, Oxon, OX11 0RH.

or by telephoning the Nirex Information Office on 0235-833009.

United Kingdom Nirex Limited is responsible for developing a deep disposal facility for Britain's solid low and intermediate-level radioactive wastes. The wastes arise from the use of nuclear technology to generate electricity, and also from industrial, medical and defence facilities in the UK.

It is estimated that a single engineered repository, in suitable geological conditions will cost from £2,500 million to build and operate for a 50 year period. It is planned that the facility will be operational soon after the turn of the century.

United Kingdom Nirex Limited

S O L U T I O N S II

TO ALL YOUR OFFICE NEEDS

Solutions, as our name implies, was formed to provide optimum results in the supply and maintenance of office systems.

We select products from the leading manufacturers' ranges, extend realistic and flexible financial packages backed up by professional account management, full on and off site maintenance, consumable supplies.

Our rapid and substantial growth is attributed to the commitment and dedication we have shown to ensuring continual support in providing practical and effective business solutions.

- **PHOTOCOPIERS**
- **TELEX TERMINALS**
- **FACSIMILE**
- **TELECOMMUNICATIONS**
- **COMPUTERS**
- **SERVICE**
- **TRAINING**
- **CONSUMABLES**

TOSHIBA Canon NEC Panasonic
Business Systems

First published in 1992

Kogan Page Ltd, 120 Pentonville Road, London N1 9JN

© Kogan Page Ltd 1992

British Cataloguing in Publication Data

A CIP record for this book is available from the British Library
ISBN 0 7494 0638 0

Typeset by DP Photosetting, Aylesbury, Bucks
Printed and bound in Great Britain by
Richard Clay Ltd, The Chaucer Press, Bungay, Suffolk.

Contents

Foreword: *Ted Wragg*   17

Introduction: *Jim Donnelly*   21

List of Contributors   25

PART ONE: THE NEW ORDER   27

1.1   Changes Resulting from LMS   29
Rowland Brown
The old order 30; the new order 30; the emphasis on
finance 31; flexibility and delegation 31

1.2   The Children Act 1989   34
Rowland Brown
Introduction 34; the impact on schools 35; reports and
material provision 37; crime prevention programmes 38;
independent schools 38; conclusion 39

PART TWO: FINANCIAL PLANNING AND BUDGETING   41

2.1   Creating the Annual Budget   43
Bruce Douglas
What is a budget? 43; the practicalities 44;
the annual cycle 48

2.2   Schools as Businesses   51
Nick Massey
Maximising assets 53; the head as managing director 53;
choosing a bank 54; using experience and advice 55

9

2.3   **Arranging Insurance**   57
       David Nichols
       What to insure 58; forward planning 62

PART THREE: HUMAN RESOURCE MANAGEMENT   63

3.1   **Heads and Deputies – Working with Governors**   65
       Mike Pugh
       The governors' meeting 65; duties and responsibilities 68;
       continuity and cohesion 70

3.2   **Appointing Staff**   71
       Brian Unwin
       Annual staffing review 75; stages of appointment and the
       preparatory steps required 77; summary and further
       considerations 82

3.3   **Staffing: Pay and Conditions**   83
       Malcolm Hewitt
       An outline pay policy 86; criteria 87;
       advertising policy 91

3.4   **Managing Staff Development**   92
       Margaret Nicholls
       Climate 92; motivation 93; access 94; organisation 94;
       finance 96; prime considerations 97; references 99

3.5   **Using Video for Professional Development**   101
       Maurice Plaskow
       INSET 101

PART FOUR: CURRICULUM MANAGEMENT   105

4.1   **Managing the Curriculum**   107
       Barry Hilditch
       Who controls the curriculum? 107; the headteacher 107;
       the governing body 108; school management 109;
       key questions to be addressed 109; the National
       Curriculum 111

Contents

PART FIVE: MARKETING AND SPONSORSHIP   113

5.1 Marketing and Public Relations for Schools   115
Laurence French
What is marketing about? 115; why market your school?
117; an outline strategy 117; communication – the heart of
the matter 121; media relations 124; the teacher as PR
practitioner 126

5.2 Sponsorship for Schools   129
Laurence French
Marketing and public relations 129; what is sponsorship?
131; sponsorship criteria 132; what have you to offer a
sponsor? 133; approaching a sponsor 135; ethical
considerations 138; legal considerations 139; professional
business managers 140; patience and perseverance 140

**PART SIX: MANAGING PROPERTY, PREMISES AND
RESOURCES**   141

6.1 Management of Buildings   143
Jim Donnelly
Schemes of delegation 143; the school maintenance budget
147; how to avoid trouble 148

6.2 Opportunities for Energy Efficiency in Schools   151
Mukund Patel
The scope for savings 151; significant factors 153;
achievements to date 157; summary 157

6.3 Energy Management in Schools   159
Jennifer Hands
Weather compensators 161; zoning 161; conclusion 161

6.4 Energy Savings in Lighting   163

6.5 Water Management   169
Derek Plimley
Money down the drain 169; investment and payback
periods 170

6.6 **Risk Management for Schools** 171
Alastair Buchan
Aims, methods and strategy 171; identification and
reduction of risk 175; levels of risk 177; your options 177;
putting your plan into action 179; conclusion 184

6.7 **Electronic Access Control** 185
Ray Hilton

6.8 **Library Security** 191
Tony Wilcox
Case study: Garth Hill Comprehensive 191; costs and
savings 192; savings are not the only benefit 193

6.9 **Closed-circuit Television** 195
Cameras 195; fixed lenses 198; site evaluation 199;
video and control signal transmission 201; control and
recording equipment 202

6.10 **Managing Resources** 205
Jim Donnelly
Allocation 205; purchase 207; repair/maintenance 210;
replacement 211; photocopiers 211

6.11 **Choosing a Desktop Laser Printer** 213
Introduction 213; connecting a laser printer: the basics
213; paper and other consumables 217; maintenance and
support 219; using a laser printer as a shared resource 220

6.12 **Contract Cleaning and Catering** 223
Jim Donnelly
Compulsory competitive tendering 223; keeping the
contract 224; catering 224; the future 225

6.13 **Management of Capital Works – Opportunities for Growth** 227
Jim Crooks
Introduction 227; background 228; function and flexibility
228; brick and block 231; brief and budget 233;
programme and progress 236; specification and
serviceability 237; the role of professional advisers 237;
choosing professional advisers 238; conclusions 239

Contents

PART SEVEN: NEW TECHNOLOGY   243

7.1   Information Technology in School Management   245
Alan Wilcox
The background 245; the need for training 246; evaluating
IT's contribution 248; a management information policy
249; the equipment 250; making best use of IT for
management 252

7.2   Computer Networking Systems Within the School   255
Brian Kennedy
Networks 255; using networks effectively 257; case study:
Dudley LEA 258; summary 262

7.3   Electronic Registration System   263
Grant Milne
Introduction 263; the existing method 264; the electronic
method 266; the advantages of electronic registration 267;
other applications of smart cards 269

PART EIGHT: EUROPE   273

8.1   European Links   275
Pat Collings
Raising awareness 275; modern foreign language teaching
276

PART NINE: USEFUL NAMES AND ADDRESSES   283

**PART TEN: DIRECTORY OF SUPPLIERS OF PRODUCTS
              AND SERVICES**   289

Index of Advertisers   331

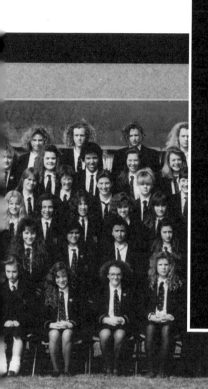

Now you can open a NatWest Account for your pupils.

Independent banking arrangements under the Local Management of Schools initiative come into effect on 1st April 1992.

To help headteachers in their expanded role, NatWest have created a specially designed financial management package.

It's the result of years of experience ·working with many schools and sponsoring educational programmes. It has been designed to be very flexible with a number of different banking facilities open to you.

We can provide a current account, help you make the most out of investing your funds, make it easier for you to manage your balances

(including an out of hours transfer and balance enquiry service) and offer you insurance advice through a dedicated schools helpline.

It's all available now through your local NatWest branch.

Speak to your local NatWest manager or call Rosemary Bevan or Denise Bell on 071-374 3270/3265, who'll be pleased to put you in touch.

Foreword

The emphasis on effective management of schools and the price of mismanagement have never been higher than they are today; several factors have combined to bring about this situation. It has not happened solely as a result of the 1988 Education Act, for government legislation throughout the 1980s has increased the management burden on senior people in schools and on governors. The 1980 Education Act required parents to be given more information, the 1981 Act redefined the rights and entitlements of those children with special educational needs, and the 1986 Act introduced teacher appraisal and reformed governing bodies. Nor have many of the management issues changed – rather they have become more important and been augmented.

To some extent the difficulty of managing a school is compounded by the unique set of circumstances in which we find ourselves. The current emphasis is on *local* management, and schools have been given more control over their budget and the way they spend their cash. Yet the curriculum for five- to 16-year-olds, the tests for children at the ages of seven, 11, 14 and 16, teachers' salaries and conditions, the formula under which money is assigned to schools – all are largely determined at *national* level.

It is the skill of managing these local and national priorities that is now at a premium, and this book tries to address the different kinds of role and competence involved. For example, few teachers or governors have the sort of financial expertise necessary to run, or even understand the running of, a budget involving between £200,000 and £2,000,000 – the range within which most school budgets fall. If priorities are to be established and implemented, salaries paid, repair bills met, books and equipment provided, plans for the future prepared, then a team of professional and lay people must work together to make sure that the money available is properly handled.

Good management, however, requires far more than the mere processing of invoices. Most school communities consist of several hundred people: the children themselves, their parents and teachers, the other employees of the school, the governors, and the local community, some of whom may use the premises outside school hours. It is a disparate and loosely bound group of older and younger people, with needs that are sometimes similar but often different. The emphasis in the late twentieth century, therefore, needs to be on management with a human face. More mechanical aspects can be left to the silicon chip.

The requirements of those who manage schools are clear for all to see. Handling a budget and dealing with people both involve an intricate process of decision-making, sometimes on broad policy matters, often on smaller detail. There is an important planning role, because if decisions are to be made on a day-to-day basis, those making them need to be aware of an overall rationale and a set of guiding principles. The strategic plan needs to be, in part at any rate, in written form so that it can be consulted, discussed, amended as necessary. For example, a school may need to give priority to science and technology one year, the expressive arts another, as the National Curriculum unfolds throughout the 1990s. But initial intentions may need to be modified in the light of changing circumstances, and the National Curriculum itself will be reviewed constantly at national as well as at local level.

If planning is the starting point, then implementing plans effectively is the testing point. The best-laid plans in the world are useless if badly applied. The tendency in recent years for schools to establish a management structure that gives as many people as feasible the chance to feel involved is one that I welcome. Research by Michael Rutter into London secondary schools in the late 1970s showed that in the more successful schools the staff felt that they had a stake in the decision-making. Once management acquires an aura of mystique, a feeling that it is something that is done to people, rather than a process in which they are involved, then its success will be limited.

Good management requires the intelligent administration of people, money, resources and strategies. It is not for the faint-hearted, nor for those unwilling to understand, take advice, act in harmony with others, or keep an open mind, while at the same time making decisions, even if some of these are difficult. Management is a blend of theory and practice, not the sort of theory untested by practicality, but rather that which can stand up to and survive the rigorous test of practical application.

I welcome the publication of *The School Management Handbook* as a valuable source of information and a compendium of practical ideas which both professional and lay people should find helpful. It certainly comes at a time when the need for effective management of schools is vital. Good intentions and Acts of Parliament are not in themselves sufficient; indeed, sometimes they are misguided. Good management is then even more important if schools are to function well and prepare the next generation of children for life in the twenty-first century.

Professor Ted Wragg
Exeter University

Introduction

The Local Management of Schools (LMS) has accelerated the acceptance of educational management as a relevant concept in schools and at the same time sharpened its focus. This has coincided with a change in the nature of management in the world of business and industry, which has come to appreciate the overarching importance of *people* in achieving its goals.

The emphasis on people is something with which schools at least feel comfortable. One does not have to speak to a teacher very long before the conversation turns to a colleague or a student: enthusiasm about their students' achievements is something with which all teachers can, as the Americans say, resonate.

Vision

A decade ago it was unusual for either businesses or schools to talk about 'vision statements'; now the terminology, at least, is recognised. Research shows the importance of senior managers in clarifying the school's vision and in setting about ensuring that it becomes reality.

Turning the vision into reality is important. Making the wish come true is the challenge for all those involved in the management of schools in the 1990s.

This book draws together the experience of those who have to put LMS into practice. It aims to help senior managers with the day-to-day practicalities of setting and achieving the visions of their own particular schools, guiding them in the requirements of the law and acting as an *aide-memoire*.

The law now impinges directly on schools in ways which it never did before. In particular, heads, deputies and governors need to know and observe legal requirements in the operation of finance, employment and the curriculum. In the first two instances, it used to be the LEA which needed to know the legal niceties, while in the case of the curriculum the law had very little to say at all until 1988.

This has all changed, as schools move towards becoming 'self-managing' institutions. Thus there is an emphasis in the book on the things you need to get right if you are to produce the effective learning institution which every school aspires to be. The writers combine a philosophy of how schools *ought* to be with an understanding of how schools *are*, to help staff and governors take their schools into the future with confidence.

Total quality management

W Edwards Deming is credited with having introduced the concept of total quality management (TQM) to the Americans. His ideas came from the way in which the Japanese rebuilt their economy after the Second World War. The philosophy of TQM is based on the involvement of all personnel in ensuring that the 'product' is as good as it can possibly be. Part of the philosophy is that one never accepts that perfection has been achieved but strives towards it nonetheless. Constantly striving for perfection, according to this view, will ensure that standards will constantly improve.

TQM is only possible if one knows what the school is trying to achieve and how one can judge this. This emphasises the need for the 'vision statement' to be clear, accepted by all and implemented by all. If it is only partially implemented the school will fall short of its own definition of quality.

Defining quality is a major task in itself. Every school will have a different definition. What will be common is a need to involve all in doing this, including students, parents and the community at large. Sometimes it is easy to feel that everyone has an opinion on the way schools should be run; in fact, very many people have a right to such an opinion!

In setting out its own definition of *quality*, the school is putting itself on the spot but equally it is then in a position to turn the theory into practical steps, which can be used as stepping-stones to the desired future. The parent considering the school for his/her child has a clear idea of what it offers; the school, in turn, knows what it wants to achieve and, hopefully, knows that it has the support of parents in what it is trying to do.

School development plans

The school development plan is the way in which a school now sets out the direction in which it wishes to move in a clear and specific way. Properly prepared – which means of necessity that all staff must be involved in its production – it allows progress to be measured and new targets to be set annually.

Development planning then becomes a continuous process of target-setting, implementation, evaluation and further target-setting, with each successive year taking the school further forward.

Many schools find it useful to set institutional targets (for example, the development of Records of Achievement): this then allows departments to set more specific targets for themselves. Provided that staff are indeed involved in setting the wider targets, they have a manageable framework within which to operate.

Flexibility is important. Five-year plans are as difficult to set and achieve in the ever-changing educational world as they are in the political and economic arenas. Annual plans, modified if necessary during the year, afford the best way of keeping the school looking to the future while not ignoring the present.

The future

One can foresee self-managing schools leading to a continual improvement in the aspiration of every school: the creation of an exciting, purposeful learning environment, which will enhance every individual in it. It is an enticing prospect. This book is one contribution to the effort.

Jim Donnelly
Litherland High School

List of Contributors

Rowland Brown is Headteacher of the Royal Grammar School, High Wycombe, Buckinghamshire. He is an acknowledged expert on education and the law.

Alastair Buchan is Assistant Director, Education Department, Sunderland Borough Council.

Pat Collings is Headteacher of Sinfin Community Comprehensive School, Derby. She is a board member of the Central Bureau for Educational Visits and Exchanges.

Jim Crooks is a construction consultant in private practice.

Jim Donnelly is Headteacher of Litherland High School, Sefton, Merseyside. He is the author of several books on educational management, including *A Handbook for Deputy Heads* and *Middle Managers in Schools and Colleges*, both published by Kogan Page.

Bruce Douglas is Headteacher of Branston School and Community College, Lincolnshire. He is a well-known writer on educational management and a regular contributor to the *Times Educational Supplement*.

Laurence French is Coordinator, Marketing and Public Relations, Campion School, Leamington Spa.

Jennifer Hands is Communications Officer for The Chartered Institution of Building Service Engineers (CIBSE).

Malcolm Hewitt is Headteacher of The Summerhill School, Dudley.

Barry Hilditch is Headteacher of Royston Comprehensive School, Barnsley.

Ray Hilton is the in-house specialist on access control for Philips Communications and Safety.

Brian Kennedy is General Adviser, Secondary IT for Dudley Local Education Authority.

Nick Massey is Schools Sector Development Manager, The Co-operative Bank.

Grant Milne is a general manager with Offcom Data Ltd.

Margaret Nicholls is Headteacher of Woodway Park Comprehensive School, Coventry.

David Nichols is Deputy Headteacher of the Park School, Nottingham.

Mukund Patel is Chief Engineer, Department of Education and Science.

Maurice Plaskow, formerly a curriculum officer with the Schools Council, set up Focus in Education in 1986 to make Video INSET packages.

Derek Plimley has worked as a consultant in the field of industrial instrumentation and control equipment.

Mike Pugh was formerly headteacher of Croesyceiliog Comprehensive School, Gwent, before becoming responsible for Governor Training for Gwent LEA. He is currently on secondment as President of the Secondary Heads' Association.

Brian Unwin was headteacher of a community comprehensive school in Clwyd. He is at present Legal Secretary of the Secondary Heads' Association.

Alan Wilcox is a former headteacher who now works with the LMS team of Dorset LEA.

Tony Wilcox is a third year management student whose project area is library systems.

Professor Ted Wragg is Director of the School of Education, University of Exeter.

Part One

The New Order

1.1

Changes Resulting from Local Management of Schools

Rowland Brown

Local Management of Schools (LMS) has brought about a change of style for the school management team as radical as the difference between the old aviator who flew the plane 'by the seat of his pants' and the modern civil jet airline pilot who has a whole crew or team in the cockpit, air traffic controllers to prescribe the route and 'high tech' all around to ensure the flight proceeds with maximum safety and predictability. Heads of mature experience will look back with a certain wistfulness to the professional association meetings of the early years of their career when distinguished veterans would rise to their feet to share their wisdom of how they had dealt with 'the Office' and seen off threats from parents or governors wanting to 'help with the running of the school', demonstrating beyond all shadow of doubt that they were captains of their ship, with all that analogy implied.

Team management styles, power-sharing, devolution in decision-taking, and corporate responsibility have become the watchwords of the 1990s. Recent legislation, in particular the Education acts of 1986 (Ss22–27) and 1988 (Ss33–47), which are the main statutory authorities for LMS, have put into print what is the spirit of the age in the organisation and structure of many public services and private industry.

The old order

Before the Education acts of 1986 and 1988 the responsibility for management of schools fitted into a structure set out in the Education Act 1944. The local authority determined the general character of the school and its place on the education map, passed regulations as to how it wished certain administrative matters to be dealt with, and determined the number of teachers a school would have and how much 'capitation' for the teaching supplies to run the school would be made available. The governors were responsible for the general conduct of the school and were regarded as the stewards of the public interest, appointed to ensure that what ought to be done was being done. The nitty gritty of management was enshrined in the phrase included in the Model Articles of Government of 1944 and well explored by the courts subsequently: 'The Head is responsible for the internal organisation, management and discipline of the school.' This phrase was virtually standard in the Articles of all schools; the courts interpreted it as giving very significant powers to heads, from deciding on matters ranging from school uniform to the shape of the school's timetable and curriculum. In a paragraph in the same section of the Articles the arrangements for appointing new teachers was customarily set out, and this often differed widely according to the philosophy of the Local Education Authority (LEA), which might or might not have sought to reserve for itself those powers and responsibilities.

The new order

LMS and the wording of the Education acts 1986 and 1988, and the cascade of Circulars and Regulations issued under authority of those acts, have shaken this pattern to the core. The checks and balances of the 1944 Act have gone; the new philosophy is that decisions about managing are best taken by those who are closest to the users of the service. In many respects now the most significant layer of authority is the governing body. S16 of the Education Act 1986 continues to require the articles of government of schools to provide for the conduct of the school to be under the direction of the governing body, reflecting the phrase dating from the 1944 Model articles. However, the role of the head has become more legislatively specified and the all-embracing phrase of the head being responsible for the internal organisation, management and discipline of the school has gone. The governing body and the head are the two prime centres of power in the running of schools, and their respective roles are now spelt out in legislative detail, in ways never encountered before in educational administrative law, in the extensive sections covering curriculum, discipline, reports and meetings in the 1986 Act,[1] and religious education, admissions, finance and school budgets, appointment and dismissal of staff in the 1988 Act.[2]

The emphasis on finance

Whereas some elements of the philosophy of LMS were in the wind in the mid 1980s, leading to the Education Act 1986, it was the Coopers and Lybrand report on the devolution of financial management of schools issued in January 1988 which pinpointed the way the delegation of this responsibility should go, and which came into effect with the 1988 Act. The report gave primacy to the allocation of individual budgets to schools and it is noteworthy that across the country governing bodies as well as many in Education Offices see LMS as being primarily about finance.

DES Circular 7/88 saw this danger and sought to impress on its readers that local management is concerned with far more than budgeting. However, the Circular in its subsequent 50 pages concerns itself almost entirely with financial and budgetary matters, reinforcing the view that the primacy of the reform is the handling of finance and resources for schools.

This Circular remains the authoritative guidance directive of the DES on LMS, and all concerned with school administration are advised to keep it within easy access if they wish to know the precise administrative wording of what is happening. It sets out the timetable for implementation – all secondary schools and all primary schools with more than 200 pupils to have delegated budgets by April 1993 – and explains how the formula for calculating budget shares is to be worked out.

Flexibility and delegation

A feature of the English and Welsh education systems has always been the way that, by having the delivery of a national provision of education effected through LEAs, there has been room for a cohesive provision and yet scope for regional variations. Metropolitan authorities, for example, traditionally kept shorter lines of communication between Education Office and schools, with closer administrative involvement than, say, those authorities which operated in rural shires with many schools considerable distances from headquarters. That particular relationship is more standardised now under the Education Act 1988, but variations of style can be effected thanks to the scope and potential for flexibility given to the relationship between governors and heads. This is particularly important in two key areas – the allocation and spending of the school's budget and the appointment of assistant staff. Once a school has a delegated budget, the power to spend it is by S36(5) of the Education Reform Act 1988 devolved to the school's governing body. The governors may delegate their power to apportion and spend this money to the head under S36(5)(b). Where a school has a strong management team and enjoys the confidence of the governors that it can most effectively handle the school's finances in the best interests of 'the purposes of the school' [S36(5)] it can be expected that this devolution to the head will apply. The governors' safeguard is that they can always withdraw that delegated authority, should this confidence prove misplaced, and the Local Authority's protection is its power to give a month's notice to the governing body of its intention to suspend having a delegated budget if the sum 'put at their disposal is not being managed for the purposes of the school in a satisfactory manner', or sooner if gross incompetence is suspected [S37 S(1) and (3)].

The process for the appointment of assistant staff is set out in Schedule 3 to the Education Reform Act 1988 in Section 2. This provides that the governing body may retain within its own remit the appointments process for assistant teachers – determining a specification for a teaching post, advertising it, conducting the interviews and making the decision on the appointment. Alternatively it may delegate the arrangements to one or more governors or devolve it to the head either on his/her own or with a governor or governors. This flexibility of practice again gives significant scope for schools to have a variety of practice, even within one Authority. The management style of a governing body with a highly active group of governors keen to involve themselves in administration will offer a different mode of operation from that of the school where the professional expertise of the head and his management team have the confidence of the board of governors.

The effects of LMS are thus to make the LEA the provider of the resources and the watchdog that what ought to be being done is being done, and the governors and head in partnership the managers of those resources. The intention behind it is the improvement in the quality and learning in schools (Circular 7/88 para. 9). Recognition of the effect of this fundamental change in school management lies at the heart of success or failure of the whole LMS initiative.

References

1 Education Act 1986. Curriculum, S17–20. Discipline, S22–27. Reports and Meetings, Ss30–32.
2 Education Act 1988. Religious education, S6–9. Admissions, S26–32. Finance and school budgets, S33–43. Appointment and dismissal of staff, S44–47 (and in particular Schedule 3).

1.2

The Children Act 1989

Rowland Brown

Introduction

This piece of legislation, which came into force on 14 October 1991, is described in Department of Health literature as the most important reform of the law concerning children this century.

Notwithstanding this claim, the word 'education' is notable by its absence from the Act, apart from the section on Education Supervision Orders [S35]. The word 'school' appears seldom, the most notable references being to the requirement of independent schools with boarding accommodation for less than 50 children to register with the local authority as a children's home [S63(5) and (6)], and the duty of proprietors of independent schools with boarding to safeguard and promote the welfare of their pupils [S87].

The themes of the 1989 Children Act (the new *vade mecum* of local authority social services departments and the courts, particularly the newly named Family Proceedings Courts and Youth Courts) are the primacy of the welfare of children, the centrality of the family units as being the best place for bringing up children wherever possible, and the emphasis on the responsibility of parents towards their children in their upbringing.

The Children Act places on local authorities a requirement to provide services for children and families in need [S17], including day care for under-fives [S18(1)] and children of school age outside

34

school hours or during school holidays [S18(5) and (6)].

It operates on the philosophy of endeavouring to create or maintain a sense of partnership between children, parents and local authorities. It gives right of appeal against court decisions, and protects the rights of parents with children being looked after by local authorities. In all cases when it comes to court proceedings, the court must put the child's welfare first in any decision-taking process.

The impact on schools

Those engaged in pastoral care in schools having pupils for whom the courts are going to be of concern, now have to be aware that criminal matters, from shoplifting to driving offences, are dealt with by the Youth Court and welfare matters are handled by the Family Proceedings Court. Whereas in the past care orders were sought in the Juvenile Court, the Children Act 1989 places these proceedings in the Family Proceedings Court, which has to assimilate many

changes in practice compared with the situation prior to 1992.

When seeking to take out an order, in every case the local authority is under an obligation to do its best to help children and their parents to stay together, but the child's welfare is the first priority. Thus if the local authority feels that a child is at risk, it may seek to take action even if the parents disagree.

Orders

Among the 14 different orders that a court can put in place according to the needs of each individual case, the ones most likely to be encountered by schools are a *supervision order* [S31], *an education supervision order* [S36], *an emergency protection order*[S44], *a child assessment order* [S43] and a *secure accommodation order* [S22(6) and (7) and S25].

The supervision order places a young person under the aegis and oversight of a social worker (and in rare cases a probation officer) if the court is of the view that the child is suffering or likely to suffer from significant harm due to a lack of parental care and control. A step up from this is the care order, where the child is placed in the care of the local authority. In a crisis, an emergency protection order can be sought (replacing the place of safety order) placing the child under the protection of the local authority for a maximum of eight days. At the top of the scale comes the secure accommodation order, which authorises the local authority to restrict the liberty of a child by keeping him or her in secure accommodation – though the dearth of such places is well known.

School pastoral staff having problems with attendance and truancy of pupils have potential recourse through the local education authority (LEA) to seek an education supervision order. It should be noted that it is the LEA which initiates the obtaining of this order, and the wording of the Act makes it clear that it is intended principally to cover the case of a registered pupil at a school not attending regularly [S36(5)(b)] and where a school attendance order issued under the Education Act 1944 [S37] has failed. Pressure to conform to the school's attendance requirements under this section of the Act is brought by the local authority putting the young person who is the subject of this order under the oversight of a supervisor who has a duty to advise, assist and befriend and give directions to both the pupil concerned and the parents. How this supervisor will succeed where welfare officers and attendance officers hitherto have not remains to be seen.

A child assessment order, made under S43, might ostensibly seem potentially to involve schools. In fact the wording of the literature accompanying the Act makes it clear that the intention of this part of the legislation is to oblige the parents to take certain steps – where they may for example have endeavoured to 'duck an issue' by failing to see that the child attends appointments at a medical clinic – to meet the requirements that are being asked of him or her so that a social worker can effectively organise an assessment of the child's physical, emotional and psychological wellbeing. The assessment orders do not emanate from schools or involve them in their preparation.

Reports and material provision

The involvement of schools in providing reports or material that may be used in the preparation of reports for the court is not changed by the Act. Section 7 of the Act states that a court may ask a local authority to arrange for one of its officers, or such other

person as the authority considers appropriate, to report to the court on matters relating to the welfare of the child; the report, as hitherto, may be made in writing, or orally, as the court requires.

Those in schools who have up till now been involved in writing or preparing reports used in court proceedings will continue to provide this service to the community. A factor to be borne in mind in the wording of the report is that the court will always keep in its collective view its obligation to recognise the primacy of the welfare of the child. When making decisions about a child and what action is appropriate at the school level, the school often has to do a balancing act between what is seen as right for it as set against what is fair for the child. The Act does not make that distinction for the court when it comes to exercising its jurisdiction in the setting of the wider community.

Crime prevention programmes

The Act lends strength and force to current moves encouraging local authorities to have crime prevention programmes and procedures to divert young people from prosecution. Schedule 2 paragraph 7 stipulates that every local authority shall take reasonable steps designed *inter alia* to encourage juveniles within its area not to commit offences and to reduce the need to bring criminal proceedings against juveniles.

The Act itself does not hint at how this is to be achieved, but the *Guidance and Regulations Volume 1* accompanying the Act advises local authorities to liaise closely with 'other agencies'; among those listed are schools and youth and community services. Schools can expect to have newly re-emphasised initiatives from their local authority to cooperate with police liaison schemes and crime prevention initiatives – all to be fitted into the already crowded years covering National Curriculum key stages 3 and 4.

Independent schools

The duty of independent schools to register as children's homes with the local authority where they provide boarding accommodation for not more than 50 children is provided for by Section 63 paragraphs 5 and 6. This does not apply to the 40 LEA schools with boarding, or to grant-maintained schools.

The Act states in Section 87 that any independent boarding school, regardless of pupil numbers, shall safeguard and promote the welfare of each child. Local authorities have a duty to 'take such steps as are reasonably practicable to enable them to determine whether the child's welfare is adequately safeguarded and promoted' – which means in effect inspection. The inspections include not only premises 'at any reasonable time' [S87(5)] but also the children and the school records, including computer records. Obstruction of an inspector in carrying out his or her duties is a criminal offence with a liability on summary conviction to a fine at level 3 on the standard scale.

If an independent school is found not to be complying with the Act, this is referred to the Secretary of State. His powers of enforcement by virtue of the Education Act 1944 SS71–3, as amended by the Children Act 1989 (Schedule 13.9), include the imposition of penalties which could lead *in extremis* to the closure of a school.

Conclusion

The Act is at pains to emphasise at all stages, and in connection with all its orders and powers, the child-centred welfare principles and the centrality of the role and responsibility of the family. Those with pastoral responsibility in schools will welcome any realistic steps that result from the Act which reverse a trend of the last quarter of a century towards placing on schools the fate of the welfare of our society.

Schools can be gratified too that the previously fragmented legislation relating to the social services and the courts is brought together in one single consistent statement of the law in the Children Act 1989.

Part Two

Financial Planning and Budgeting

Creating the Annual Budget

Bruce Douglas

What is a budget?

It is 'the expression, in monetary terms, of an institution's plans for a given period, and for given price assumptions.' Contemplation of that typical definition will lead to some very important deductions about budgeting.

First, paradoxical though it may seem, a budget is not about money. Though composed of a list of amounts of money allocated, it is, first and foremost, as the definition says, an expression of *plans*. And those plans are not about money, they are to do with the activities of teaching and learning, and with the personnel, premises, consumables and services required to make these plans happen. The budget is the place where everything is quantified and then costed, but it is the educational activity which drives the budget, not the other way round.

We sometimes pretend the opposite in order to emphasise that we could plan more ambitiously if better resourced, but lack of money does create real educational restraints. Indeed one of our roles as heads and deputies (who else has the authoritative knowledge to perform it?) is to state good reasons why we need more for young people's education. But when we sit down to write a budget, asking for more is not in our minds. Deciding what educational activities can and will happen, certainly is. Educational budgeting is an educationally creative task, unless we choose to describe as 'budgeting' only that final part of the process, where educational planning has already taken place, the curriculum has been decided, the staff allocated, and all that is left is to calculate how much exactly the listed teachers, rooms and supplies will cost.

That is a large enough task, and budgeting always ends there, but the wider definition does keep before us the important truth that the choices individual teachers or departments make, out of educational conviction, through a wider consensus, or in response to institutional or national requirements, are choices whose forward costing produces the budget.

So the introduction of drama instead of home economics; or the abandonment of drama in favour of science; the buying of scientific instruments instead of tennis nets; the replacement of tennis nets instead of computers – all such decisions, and a thousand more, which are the stuff of school development, are daily, weekly, yearly, writing the budget. All are subject to the educational visions (and the power games) that schools contain. Therefore those who make those decisions really 'control' the budget.

In a profession like teaching, where collegiality is a way of life, it is perhaps as well to remind ourselves and others that the new emphasis on institutional costing that Local Management of Schools (LMS) has created is not necessarily a threat to that tradition.

Not that there is therefore an easy, sentimental way of creating a budget which everybody owns. A professional consensus, and a consensus between professional and lay bodies (especially the governing bodies), is generally largely in place (ie mostly schools agree that most of what they do is right). But the professional debate is splendidly ferocious at the margin, and lay–professional togetherness has to be won, by explanation, two-way listening, mutual respect and compromise.

Budgets really are costed future plans, and since both education and schools are as complex as they are, the plans won't come easily.

The practicalities

Costing the plans: listing the costs

First ask, 'are *all* plans identified and listed?' At the start of LMS it was found ridiculously easy to overlook some items.

The major cost, staffing, arising naturally out of the time-tabler's art of specifying how many teacher periods of each subject are needed, is produced by a systematic working through of the projected curriculum, but it is rather easier, for example, to overlook *services* you require, and have no intention of *doing without*, though they may not be in your mind. Typically, in the early days, the first wave of schools produced examples of 'forgetting' (or perhaps 'not realising') that of course they wanted dustbins emptied, cookers serviced, premises annually spring-cleaned in the holidays.

They also forgot that they planned (ie wanted) to retain depreciating assets. Five extra computers are always costed, but the fact that the replacement life of the 25 already in use means another five should be budgeted for might slip past. The tennis court surround-fence may not even need patching *this* year, but if it has a 15-year life span, and a cost of £30,000, you had better 'plan' somehow to 'reserve' £2000 a year for its upkeep.

Furniture is a particular problem. Just what *is* the expected life span in this school of this quality of chair? A look at the throw-out rate (does the caretaker know it?) might provide a clue.

LMS itself is ensuring that a 'last year's list' of costings will be available, so preventing the overlooking of important costs. For schools new to delegated budgeting, a glance at the budgets of a couple of schools of similar size will be of immense help, though the percentage allocations to different headings may not be identical, either because of real cost differences (School A costs £10,000 more to heat to the same temperature than School B with the same Numbers on Roll (NOR)) or because of a difference in categorising (School A counts the caretaker as a non-teaching staff cost, School B counts him or her as a premises cost). However, more and more, as previous budgets become available, the annual cycle can focus mainly on changes.

So, the latter stage of budget creation, after plans are made, is the methodical writing down of lists of the implied activities/supplies/ services, first making sure that the list is *complete*, and pondering over how the *annual* cost can be estimated/identified, and from what sources of information.

Pay and price changes

The price base constantly shifts: inflation happens; pay increases are awarded. It helps to choose an understood price base (eg the

'November price base' used by most LEAs) if you are using, as you will, a previous year's budget as a guide for the next. You can simply apply the current price plus an estimate for inflation during the year (but remember an estimated 10 per cent increase by the end of the year does not mean a 10 per cent increase for your budget, if some of it is spent before the end of the year). Most of this is methodical common sense, plus informed guesswork (eg on fuel prices) but the most important point about inflation is to remember that it happens, and to make allowances.

Quantity changes

Sensible use of last year's budget involves asking 'what is different' not just in price, but also in quantity. Because schools continually develop, so do the *proportions of activities* represented in the budget. A change in the curriculum may mean more science, less drama staffing (and of course, even though the cost in pounds may be the same, the personnel change needs careful management, to say the least!) These 'quantity' changes are most likely to relate to curriculum change, change in use or area of premises, and changes in NOR.

Focus on such changes enables us most easily to make use of previous budgets, by adjusting the quantities required for our future plans. Assuming we also retain an awareness of price changes, and put those into the sums, we can often stay on course. But not always. Sometimes after costing changes we find we are *disproportionately* better or worse off than before. This is because of fluctuations in income.

Income fluctuation

Income (the other starting point for budgets) is of course derived from the local LMS formula, which is largely, but not entirely, related to NOR. It is because costs are also largely, but not entirely so related, that LMS budgets are possible, but when the two 'not entirelys' do not cancel each other out, there is a sudden deficit (or windfall).

This is *not* the perennial 'deficit' between anticipated income and desirable (but unfortunately unrealistic) expenditure. Part of the earlier process will be to gain a rough idea of how many of our desired plans can be afforded, and the plans will have been

prioritised and modified (five new computers, not ten, four rooms redecorated, not eight, one teacher for that 'A' level Geography group of 22, not two, no satellite receiver dish, no bursar).

Often that prioritising is within categories which have strategic limits (eg there is an annual Information Technology (IT) expansion budget, so those five new computers beat the claims of other IT equipment, but could not trespass on the redecoration budget; there is a staffing number of norm, such as a historic pupil-teacher ratio, so that Geography 'A' level demand for eight extra teacher periods was prioritised against the wish to split a large Year 10 science class but not, without debate on recosting strategic allocations, against the school caretaking or cleaning or books budget). All that kind of adjustment goes on, much of it not even reaching the governing body, except as reports of final decisions or proposals within governor-agreed strategic norms.

However, a change in NOR may lead to a disproportionate loss or increase in LMS income (eg if a small-school allowance in the formula is gained or lost). More critically, school *costs* may not alter in line with NOR fluctuations. A few students more (or less) can alter dramatically the number of teachers required, as class size thresholds are passed. The loss of 40 6th formers and 100K of income could reduce group size but leave *no* 'A' level group empty enough to collapse (real loss of spending power of about 100K). Moreover, a school typically has 'fixed' premises costs (rates, heating, telephones, etc) and almost always will be *worse* off if NOR falls below capacity. When LEAs paid premises costs, this was a uniform tax on all schools; now it falls on the particular case.

So the same *budget* build process, based on the *same* curriculum, might 'work' one year and not the next. The moral is to know your local scheme well, to know its thresholds (and those of the school) and to plan and calculate *ahead*, because fluctuations, even if not changeable, might be spreadable over several years if foreseen (but are perhaps unmanageable if not).

The annual cycle

Finally, who works all this out, and when? Granted that everyone is in fact debating plans all the time, there must be decision-moments when next year's plans are fixed, so that, from then, the continuing debate refers to following years. There must also be times for formal presentation to, discussion with, and approval by, governing bodies.

Typically, the governing body, though no doubt aware of and involved in ongoing ideas for development, will have a formal curriculum plan presented (often to a committee) in January/February, accompanied then or briefly afterwards by a staffing plan and a staffing number (at which time it can review its strategic norms for staffing). Any foreseen staffing problems (eg recruitment or redundancy) will need action to be started at once.

A draft budget, based on that curriculum and staffing, and on an assumed pay and prices increase can be presented (again probably to a committee) around February (incorporating of course an estimate of LMS formula income). Any special projects or final priorities can be discussed. If approved, this budget framework can be refined and presented as a full budget in March/April, ready to send to the LEA (if a maintained school) in April/May.

CHECKLIST

1. Know your educational plans. They, and those who form them, form the budget.

2. Identify *all* plans for costing (including unspoken plans to maintain depreciating assets such as furniture, equipment, tennis courts, labs, office machinery).

3. Alert governing body if you want to propose adjustment to strategic norms.

4. Cost your plans – previous costs are a guide but:
   - Decide on a sensible level of reserves (5%?) and try to build that in.
   - Remember to adjust for *price changes* from last year to date, and from now to the following year-end. It helps to show pay and price assumptions separately.
   - Remember to adjust for *quantity changes*, trying to keep cost/changes in line with NOR. This is difficult, though you can try applying NOR to such items as departmental capitation, or minutes of support time, etc, per pupil.
   - Cost each staff member individually, not forgetting increments, allowances, on-costs, pay increases (often staged).

5. Identify any disproportionate rises/falls in costs (eg class-size thresholds passed, causing larger than pro-rata additions/reductions in staffing on the current curriculum).

6. Apply NOR to current local LMS formula to produce 'income'. Check for any formula changes or thresholds crossed (eg small-school allowance gained or lost). Check if LMS budget (corrected for inflation) is up or down in line with NOR.

7. Match 4 to 6. Alert everyone if the costs/income match is different from last year and make plans to deal with windfalls/deficits not arising out of *your* educational planning.

8. Formally present, discuss, if necessary modify, gain approval.

9. Start planning for next year and the year after.

Further reading

A fuller account of budgeting, with a 'real' budget included, and examples of cash flow management, is given in Douglas, B., *Managing The School Budget*, The Secondary Heads' Association, Regent Road, Leicester LE1 7PG, £6.50.

Schools as Businesses

Nick Massey

The new Managing Director sat down to wait for the Bank Manager. He was nervous, but who wouldn't be when he's outlining the plans for his first business venture?

He considered the sort of questions the Bank Manager would be asking, and mentally rehearsed his answers:

'*What sort of business are you in?*'
'It's a service industry.'
'*Expected turnover?*'
'We'll control around £1,000,000 in the first year.'
'*Where is your business?*'
'It's just up the road from here, on the edge of the large housing estate.'
'*A new building?*'
'Quite new. The owner looked after the building pretty well, but now we are responsible for the maintenance.'
'*This service of yours, is demand high?*'
'Yes but it's a competitive field so we have to make our standards high too.'
'*Who are your customers?*'
'Our principal customers are local families, but we aim to diversify by offering leisure facilities, translation and foreign language training for local companies, leasing time on our computer system, and operating a drama studio with audio-visual facilities for use by local drama organisations. We're also looking

at operating a pre-school nursery facility for working mums. *'Yes, but what's your core business?'*

His thoughts were interrupted by the arrival of the Bank Manager. The Managing Director introduced himself:

'Good morning. I'm Mr Jones, the headmaster of the High School, and I'd like to talk to you about how we're going to do business in the future . . .

That's a scene which will be enacted time and again as headteachers and governors go to the banks to meet the demands of Local Management of Schools (LMS).

Maximising assets

'School Enterprises' will be the small business boom of the decade if the Government has its way. This is because it sees acceptable standards of education going hand-in-hand with efficient management and making the most of the school's resources – both physical and financial.

Schools have the chance to get off to a flying start in the business stakes. After all they are invariably well-placed, close to their customers. They also have an established customer base on which to build, and ready-made facilities for pursuing the business of education; facilities which are often used for just six hours of the day, and stand idle at evenings, weekends and holidays.

The school's budget is initially set by a formula produced by the Government and dependent mainly on the numbers of pupils at the school. If the school can find ways of increasing its income, that money can be used to enhance the educational facilities and opportunities for its pupils. So it's in the interests of everyone at the school to work at ensuring they make the most of the money they receive, and the money they can earn through other sources, such as those outlined earlier by our model 'Managing Director'.

The head as 'Managing Director'

Under LMS the head teacher of even a small secondary school could be handling a non-staff budget of £300,000 a year. Delegated budgets for larger schools can run into millions. The head will also have the responsibility for recruiting and managing the school's staff at all levels, although the actual salaries will still be paid direct by the LEA. And as the 'Managing Director' of High School Enterprises with the backing of the Board (of governors) it will be the head's job to ensure the school and its pupils (or should it be shareholders?) profit from the running of the whole operation.

The head will have to assemble a senior management team. A bursar, who takes the role of finance director, a company secretary, and a marketing manager, are just some of the positions which will have to be filled. Some schools have already appointed full-time business managers to make the most of LMS; many others are using the skills available both from their own staff, and among governors and parents.

But it is the headteacher and the members of the senior management team who must take the brunt of the responsibility, and headteachers across the country admit they need all the help they can get to manage their new responsibilities and their own 'core business' of running their school effectively.

Choosing a bank

Strong support from a local bank should be a vital factor in the success of any 'education enterprise', whether it is a secondary school taking financial control under LMS, a school which has opted out to achieve grant maintained status, an independent school, or a special school. The experiences of schools which have already chosen a bank have demonstrated one basic rule – it pays to shop around. Schools should talk to the banks to discover not only who wants their business, but who can best serve it; that doesn't always mean the nearest available High Street branch.

The most telling change for many schools will be taking control of their own purse strings by having their own cheque book. But whose cheque book and what type of account will best serve the school?

Schools should be seeking an interest-bearing cheque account so that they gain from the substantial balances which may remain in their account. A school could, for example, receive its budget in three instalments during the financial year – that means our model school could find itself with £100,000 sitting in its account at any one time. That money should be earning interest.

There should also be rapid transfer of funds from the LEA to the school. Posting a cheque, then awaiting clearance could mean, on £100,000, the loss of £200 to £300 interest in less than a week! How many books can a school buy with that?

The cost of services such as cheques or transactions should be assessed, and balanced against the practical advice and guidance the Bank Manager is willing to give.

Desktop banking, which gives the school direct access to its accounts through its own computer, is a desirable option, because that means that funds can be shifted to higher interest accounts, transactions checked and information obtained on a 24-hour basis.

Other additional services should also be carefully considered such as secure cash-collection – to avoid the physical risk and high insurance premiums which go with making a regular trip to the bank with a bag of money.

Using experience and advice

Schools might also look for banks which already have experience of education through their involvement with private schools or nurseries, or local authorities; after all there's nothing quite like the gift of hindsight when it comes to sorting out problems or meeting special needs.

Teachers and governors should be ready to accept constructive advice as they start to go through the learning curve in balancing the books and making the most of money and other assets. Above all, school managers shouldn't be afraid to demand from banks a service which is more than simply a make-do package plucked off the shelf of standard accounts and services. Schools now mean business, and so should the banks which handle their money.

We'll keep you covered . . . whatever happens.

As a Bursar or Headteacher you provide the pupils in your care with an education of the best possible standard.

As the specialists in education insurance Holmwoods are prepared to accept a similar level of responsibility with regard to your insurances.

Our extremely competitive tailor-made schools policy provides comprehensive cover to tackle your special needs.

We would be delighted to help you with:

- Building and Contents
- Consequential Loss
- Public and Employers Liability
- Governors Liability
- Motor
- Travel
- Pupils' Personal Accident
- Supply Teachers
- Fidelity

Holmwoods
9-17 Perrymount Road
Haywards Heath
West Sussex RH16 1TA
Telephone (0444) 458144

Holmwoods
THE SPECIALISTS IN EDUCATION INSURANCE
A member of the Brown Shipley Group

60 YEARS IN THE SCHOOLS INSURANCE MARKET
INSURANCE BROKERS TO OVER 1000 SCHOOLS

2.3

Arranging Insurance

David Nichols

Each Local Education Authority (LEA) has considerable discretion as to the degree to which responsibility for insurance is delegated to schools or retained under central control. In practice LEAs are usually very keen and able to provide support and advice to the schools they maintain. Schools which are not maintained by an LEA obviously do not have the opportunity to participate in these centrally negotiated arrangements and must arrange their own cover in all areas.

When first considering insurance the following steps should be taken:

1. Governors and budget managers should make contact with the LEA's Insurance Department to ascertain which elements of insurance are covered by centrally negotiated and funded policies and which are left to the discretion of individual schools.

2. Two lists should then be drawn up; one noting all forms of insurance which are provided automatically by the LEA and the second detailing all forms of risk for which the school itself, through its governors, is responsible.

3. Advice should be sought as to whether the LEA has negotiated any group purchase arrangements for those aspects of insurance which have been delegated to schools. Such arrangements can usually offer considerable savings on

premiums when compared with individually negotiated packages. It is however, always worth obtaining independent quotes from reputable insurers to provide a comparison.

4. Advice should be sought as to which insurance companies offer the most suitable packages where no centrally negotiated policy exists.

What to insure

The major areas requiring insurance fall into the following categories:

Buildings and contents

Generally the LEA insures centrally for structural damage and repairs, leaving the smaller items, such as glazing, plumbing, interior and exterior decoration and minor roof repairs to the individual school. The LEA retains responsibility for any large machinery or plant on school premises.

The exact division between that for which the school is responsible and that for which the LEA is responsible varies considerably. It is important therefore that governors and budget managers are absolutely clear as to the extent of their liability. Most LEAs publish a document setting out exactly where responsibility lies, for all aspects of building maintenance from curtain tracks to filtration systems for swimming pools.

Schools which derive a high income from public lettings should also ascertain whether they are insured through the LEA for consequential loss should buildings be rendered unusable for a prolonged period.

All fixtures, fittings and contents are the school's responsibility and it is normal to arrange an 'All Perils' policy to cover buildings and contents. This is likely to be the most expensive essential insurance item delegated to a school and many LEAs have negotiated their own reduced premium schemes which can offer good value.

There are also policies available to cover any specific, high-cost items, such as computers and audio-visual equipment, which may be excluded from the general policy. It is important for the budget manager to be aware of exactly what any policy does cover and to consider whether it is worth insuring those items which are excluded.

One aspect to check is the extent, if any, to which the personal belongings of staff, governors and visitors are covered on school premises.

Most buildings and contents policies carry an excess, the level of which may influence a decision on insuring individual items.

Public and employer's liability

It is normal practice for LEAs to take out a central policy to cover both public liability and employer's liability. Governing bodies need to ascertain that they are covered by such a policy and, if not, to effect cover immediately.

These policies will generally include cover for such risks as professional negligence, slander and libel. The delegated powers now possessed by governors and headteachers increase the possibility of their being subject to civil action, so this is a priority area.

Fidelity guarantee

Here again the LEA is likely to insure all its staff centrally against fraud or 'infidelity'. The governors need to ensure that they are also covered by this policy. It is also a good idea to examine whether it has been, or could be, extended to cover non-public funds and the Parent-Teacher Association (PTA).

Legal costs

As employer, the LEA takes responsibility for legal costs involved in defending actions for unfair dismissal and for issues concerning employment legislation.

An individual school will not normally need to purchase insurance for these purposes, although governors should check with their LEA that they are covered for actions against them concerning the operation of pay and promotion policies within the school.

Personal accident

While this form of insurance is usually provided by the LEA the extent and detail varies considerably. It is therefore worthwhile examining exactly what has been provided and considering whether the governing body wishes to augment this cover.

The four main categories to check are:

1. staff, teaching and non-teaching, within school, on extra-curricular and off-site activities and travelling to and from school;

2. governors on school duties;

3. visitors and volunteer workers within school;

4. pupils within school, on extra-curricular and off-site activities and on work-experience placements.

It is worth noting that some schools are encouraging parents to insure their own children.

PTA and public access events

Under LMS schools are moving more and more towards generating their own income. When large events are held involving public access and/or the handling of large amounts of cash, the need for insurance is self-evident.

PTAs have traditionally arranged their own insurance, but this may now be unnecessary as many LEA-organised policies already applied to schools include such fund-raising events in their schedules as normal school activities. This certainly merits investigation by governors and the PTA as it could lead to savings.

School trips

While LEAs will mostly be found to cover all their staff against accidents and other problems incurred while exercising their professional duties in or out of school, this is not normally the case with pupils. The only exception to this is if the accident or injury occurs as a result of negligence by the school or its staff.

It is therefore important that, when planning trips over any considerable distance or period, schools should check on what type of cover is necessary and what is available. There are many options and, while travel companies will usually offer a competitive all-in package, it is essential to examine the small print, check on any excess payable and seek alternative quotes for comparison.

The principal categories to check for cover are:

1. personal accident/illness;

2. loss of, or damage to, belongings;

3. vehicles owned by the party, including provision for breakdown.

Contractors

Schools should ensure that any contractor employed upon their premises has a suitable public liability insurance policy. As a rough guideline, such a policy should allow for a minimum of £2 million cover where major works are concerned and £1 million for all minor works.

In practice most reputable contractors do carry this kind of policy, but it is in the school's interest to ensure that this is so in all cases.

Cover for absent staff

An interesting one! In the heady early days of LMS, brokers and insurance companies were keen to get in on the act, often offering amazingly low premiums. Fingers were burned and the approach is now rather more sober, with higher premiums.

Many LEAs have negotiated a central package with an insurance company, for paying for supply teachers to cover for absent staff for a fixed period of time, eg from the third to the twentieth day of absence. The exact details vary, as does the amount paid out per day of cover. The premiums are usually calculated on a set figure per member of staff on the school's establishment.

There are also independently operated schemes which may be worth consideration.

Some schools have chosen to gamble on a healthy staff and have placed a sum equivalent to the insurance premium into a contingency fund for supply cover in the hope that much of it will not be used. This clearly is the sort of gamble which insurance seeks to avoid, but a school which gambles luckily can save a fair amount. For example, 58 members of staff at an annual premium of, say, £125, adds up to £7,250. Clearly this is an issue which many governing bodies will want to discuss.

Forward planning

When the school has decided the extent of its needs, care needs to be taken to establish when policies become operative and when they are renewable. It should also be recorded when premiums will be payable and exactly how much is involved in each policy, as the cost manager will need to calculate a total projected insurance budget well before 1 April each year in order to set an accurate budget.

CHECKLIST OF INSURANCE CATEGORIES

- Buildings and contents
- Public liability and
  employer's liability
- Fidelity guarantee
- Legal costs
- Personal accident
- PTA and public
  access events
- School trips
- Contractors
- Cover for absent
  staff

Part Three

Human Resource Management

Heads and Deputies – Working with Governors

Mike Pugh

'Finally we have the governors – no problem there, keep the chairman sweet, meet them as rarely as possible, tell them nothing important, and give them front row reserves seats for all school performances.' Thus concluded a long tirade from an old but not entirely wise headteacher expounding to me his management style in the early 1980s. It was not good advice then, and would be a recipe for disaster today. The new – post 1988 – governors have a right and a need to know about their school in detail if they are to carry out their duties and responsibilities successfully. Teamwork, partnership and sharing between heads and the governing body are essential. Such are the powers of governors that where this vital relationship breaks down, pupils are bound to suffer, and the very livelihood of the head can be at risk.

The governors' meeting

The headteacher is the person most likely to be in a position to lead in creating an effective team and he or she should be prepared to accept the challenge.

An efficient governing body will be:

1. A group of equal partners, confident and relaxed in each others' company, with no second-class members.

2. An arena where all available skills and experiences are fully utilised, and self-belief flourishes.

3. A group where full information is available to all.

4. Well organised:
    - minutes and agendas always available at least a week before any meeting;
    - topics for discussion based on school needs, not LEA demands;
    - head and chairman hold a pre-meeting review of the agenda;
    - consensus-seeking is the norm, not public or private voting to resolve issues;
    - except in emergencies, an agreed finishing time is determined, perhaps based on a timed or prioritised agenda.
    - recognition that these are business meetings to be treated as such.

5. Prudent in having a deputy head in attendance. Many governing bodies have been thrown into chaos when a

strong headteacher falls by the wayside through accident, illness, or worse. Suitable cover must be available.

6. Agreed on a common purpose, shared values, clear aims, and procedures for coping with important issues as they arise.

7. A group where the headteacher sees the sensitive management and guidance of governors as being just as important as he/she does the management of staff and pupils.

8. Determined to support the school, the staff and the pupils, and to present them in the best possible light to the local community. At the same time it will never fail to query if it feels that certain aspects of school organisation, work, or achievement are less successful than they might be.

Training

Even the most effective governing bodies need a planned programme of quality, on-going training, mostly derived from the head and the teaching staff, not from LEA support or training officers. This is because, in order to carry out their specific duties and responsibilities, governors must know their school and its workings in detail, and no outsider can possibly provide the necessary information. Heads should not dominate these sessions but invite staff colleagues to describe their work to governors. Often subject-based, such presentations could also include special needs provision, careers guidance, or pastoral care planning. An agenda slot of perhaps 10–15 minutes should be available at each full meeting. LEA training will often be of the large-scale area variety, and should not be ignored, since it can provide useful broad-brush advice on major topics, but heads must prepare for the fact that by mid-1992 it is likely that at least 50 per cent of all monies specifically earmarked for training governors will be paid direct to schools, thus enabling them to establish training exactly to match the perceived needs.

All training for governors must be supplemented by practical hands-on experience, best achieved by regular small-group visits to the school. Initial reticence can be overcome if governors feel that they are welcome in classrooms. However such visits *must*:

1. Be agreed well in advance with the headteacher.

2. Be accepted by the staff likely to be involved.

3. Be organised and purposeful – just popping in to see that everything is all right is not acceptable.

4. Offer governors specific roles to adopt. One of them may have already accepted responsibility for monitoring special needs and could thus focus attention on that area. Others could adopt a class, shadow a particular pupil for a morning, or try to become an expert within one subject department, even staying with the headteacher for a day.

5. Result in governors knowing at least a little more about the complicated structures which make up their school, and ideally give teachers an enhanced knowledge and acceptance of the sort of people who are now charged with helping to run the school.

Governors might also be invited to attend staff meetings and INSET Days, as well as the usual plays, concerts, etc.

Most governors are keen and willing to learn. Proper training will enable them to make better, more informed decisions which can only benefit the school and its pupils.

Duties and responsibilities

The initial DES list of some 20 duties and responsibilities caused considerable concern, including as it did such exotica as ensuring that the National Curriculum was taught and appropriately tested, that the school had policies for discipline, special needs, and health and sex education, that RE and a daily act of corporate worship – mainly Christian in character – were provided, and that an annual report was prepared for parents prior to their invitation to an Annual Meeting. The supervision and monitoring of the school budget via local management was later added to this comprehensive list. Heads must convince governors that it is not their role to examine these areas in microscopic detail nor to embark on a wholesale review, revamping, and rewriting of long established, known-to-be-successful, school policy documents. The American adage of 'If a thing works, don't fix it' is good advice. However, if in any of these areas individual governors are worried or concerned, they must feel completely free to seek answers. These should always come initially from the headteacher, but if this proves unsatisfactory, the governing body should be involved.

Heads should regularly remind governors that power brings responsibilities not always of a pleasant nature. They may have to decide on the redundancy of a popular member of staff, or take disciplinary action against a long-serving teacher. Heads confronted by weak governors must not agree to go it alone on such issues. Teamwork and partnership applies to the bad as well as the good news of governorship. Governors should recognise that on such occasions:

1. LEA advice, of a legal or general kind, is normally available.

2. Their lifeline is that they acted in good faith on all the evidence available and are therefore unlikely to be liable for the consequences.

3. It is essential to have known and agreed procedures for action in several extremely important areas:
    - staff appointments;
    - pupil exclusions;
    - staff salaries and conditions of service;
    - dealing with appeals and complaints;
    - coping with LMS;
    - pupil admissions (agreed with the LEA).

    Such procedures should be in place in anticipation of possible future happenings, not hastily cobbled together when a crisis is already in existence.

If they are founded on the correct legal base, and can be seen to be both fair and sensible, then much trouble is likely to be avoided. Trouble, which can often become public, may upset the smooth running of the school. Governors, guided by the head, should seek to be known as good employers. To establish such procedures may encourage the formulation of governor sub-committees. A widely used tactic, this has the benefits of sharing out an ever-increasing workload, and using to the full specific skills and experiences of individual governors. Once again certain aspects should be carefully considered in advance.

1. The size and composition of these groups.

2. Have they been properly established – agreed by 75 per cent of the full governing body, for example?

3. How often will they meet?

4. Have they a clear remit or will the work of one Committee –
    Appointments perhaps – overlap into that of another –
    Finance – and cause confusion?

5. Are their powers of decision-making clearly defined and
    understood by non-Committee members?

6. Have reporting-back facilities been set up?

7. Do you intend to have the head, a deputy, or member of
    teaching staff as a Committee Chair? Don't – it's illegal.

8. Is equal importance to be given to all Committees? Many a
    good governing body has been spoiled by an apparently all-
    powerful Finance Committee beginning to dominate
    proceedings.

Continuity and cohesion

Finally, the successful governing body, prompted by the headteacher, will always be looking to the future. With a four-year
tenure of office, and many governors facing re-election in 1992,
plans should be laid to ensure that first-rate governors are not
unceremoniously removed. To build an almost totally new set of
governors every four years is not sensible. The area which offers
flexibility is that of co-opted governors where parents whose
children have left the school can be re-elected in this new guise, as
can local persons who have long shown a sincere interest in the
school and its workings.

Above all there is the task of convincing governors that despite all
the hard work, the difficult decision-making, the occasional hurtful
press headlines, the criticism of colleagues in the local community,
being a governor is – as it never used to be – work of vital
importance where an effective team really can influence the school
life and work of pupils and help to enable them to develop their
potential to the full. Could anything be more worthwhile or
fulfilling?

3.2

Appointing Staff

Brian Unwin

The key principles of making appointments to the staff of the school (both teaching and non-teaching) remain as they have been for many years, but the process by which the selectors choose the person who will best do the job is now regulated by statute. The context, the regulations and procedures have now significantly changed as a result of the Education Reform Act 1988 (ERA). These changes have shifted the responsibility for making appointments to the governing body of delegated, maintained schools, grant maintained schools and city technology colleges. The latter two categories have some additional powers and responsibilities.

For maintained schools, where the governors are the 'relevant body', two documents must guide and inform their arrangements for making appointments to the school (this includes the appointment of external candidates and internal appointments and promotions).

First, there is Schedule 3 of ERA. This sets out the requirements for:

- the appointment of headteachers and deputy headteachers, including the arrangements and composition of the selection panel and its relationship with the whole governing body and the requirement to advertise;

- the appointment of other teachers, including the occasions when an advertisement is required, the position of candidates nominated by the LEA, the requirement, provided the

SEATS OF LEARNING

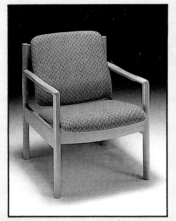

Posture 773   Modula 749

ERCOL is a UK manufacturer of solid wood furniture and upholstery supplying all Government educational establishments, i.e. universities, polytechnics, colleges and schools, and our contract furniture meets the British Standard requirements for severe contract use for strength and flame retardancy.

There are four ranges:

MODULA — a range of loose cushioned chairs and matching tables.

POSTURE — an aesthetically appealing range of fixed seat chairs designed to give years of trouble free use.

MANDEVILLE — a range of high-seated chairs most suitable for back sufferers, the elderly and post-operative.

LIFESTYLE — a range of craftsman made, hand finished furniture suitable for both the retail and contract market.

Catalogues, leaflets and price lists are obtainable on request.

Ercol Contracts Marketing Division
High Wycombe, Buckinghamshire. HP13 7AE Telephone 0494 521261 Fax 0494 462467

selected candidate is qualified, for the LEA to appoint the selected person;

- the power for the governors to delegate the function of appointment to one or more governors, the headteacher or one or more governors and the headteacher acting together;

- the advice of the chief education officer (CEO) and the headteacher, including the entitlement to be present at *all* procedures to give advice; in the case of headship and deputy headship appointments it is the duty of the CEO to give advice whether asked or not; in other appointments, the duty is to give advice if so requested.

  The governing body or delegated individuals or group must consider that advice. It is critical that such consideration should be clearly minuted and, if rejected, reasons given. On this will rest the success of the defence of acting in good faith.

- appointments of non-teaching staff, including consideration of matters to be sent on to the LEA, and the consultation with the head;

- the appointment of clerk to the governing body.

Second, there is the School Government Regulations 1989 Statutory Instrument 1503.

If the governing body chooses to make appointments by using the arrangements outlined in Regulations 25 and 26, they must conform to the detailed procedures that require a quorum of 75 per cent of the *full governing body.*

It is under Regulation 25 that the governing body will determine its policies relating to matters of appointment procedures (determination of the delegation to individuals or groups, grades, etc).

The context to making all appointments, including upgradings, will normally include:

The school development plan

In effect, this will be the strategic plan for the school for the next few years, containing within the plan the next year, the middle view, and the longer view. It is likely to include a view of staffing structures and grades appropriate to the functions set out in the structure.

The governors' policy on pay

This establishes, in a policy statement, the governing body's intention to be a good employer, and as such, addressing the issues of recruitment, retention, promotion and professional development. This policy should be in sufficient detail to establish criteria for grades, recruitment point on the standard scale, the appropriate point on the spine for heads and deputies, criteria for the use of discretions – incremental progression, incremental enhancement, level and numbers of incentives allowing discretionary scale points (the current Teachers' Pay and Conditions Document and accompanying Circular and any successor documents). For non-teaching staff, the appopriate pay scales and advisory documents from the Local Authorities' Conditions of Service Advisory Board.

The governors' employment powers relevant to appointment

Two circulars on LMS, DES 7/88 – Education Reform Act: Local

Management of Schools (paragraphs 157–164) and DES 7/91 – Local Management of Schools: Further Guidance (paragraphs 46–48) set out in a different form the governing body's duties and responsibilities in relation to appointments:

- to set the number of staff employed (teaching and non-teaching);

- to establish the appropriate procedures within the regulations;

- to appoint and determine salary levels within the arrangements set out in the relevant national agreements;

- to use, as they determine, any discretions that the governing body has.

Heads and deputies need to ensure that they are familiar with the framework and details of the policy, procedures, powers and responsibilities that exist and particularly the relationship between the governing body and the LEA who holds and services the contracts of staff.

In making appointments, the governing body must be made aware of its responsibilities to observe the requirements of the following legislation:

- Race Relations Act 1976

- Equal Pay Act 1970

- Sex Discrimination Act 1975

- Trade Union and Labour Relations Act 1974

Annual staffing review

In order that decisions on staffing are made on the most up-to-date information, a formal review should take place each year so that the pupil numbers and curriculum needs can be analysed and put against the existing staff and curriculum. This will inform decisions relating to the setting of staffing levels but particularly on whether vacancies that occur should be recruited on the basis of the present arrangements or on a new job specification. All this needs to be matched against the budget.

Stages of appointment and the preparatory steps required

– Advance preparation	– Shortlisting
– Vacancy analysis	– Arrangements for interview
– Check effective potential salary costs	– Interview questions
	– Decision
– Job description and post-holder specification	– Confirmation of offer and information to the LEA
– Advertisement	

Table 3.2.1 *Checklist of procedures for appointing staff*

Advance preparation

Have ready:

- Application forms: These set out information that will help heads and deputies to establish basic salary costs;

- Declaration form for spent convictions for shortlisted candidates where they will have close contact with children;

- School information and specifications to be sent to candidates.

Vacancy analysis

1. Establish who does this: the head alone or with a committee?

2. Considerations: conclusion from the staffing review.

3. Questions:
    - What are the staffing priorities of the school?
    - What jobs need doing?
    - Should the vacancy be:
        - advertised as a direct replacement?
        - a different post? If so, what?
        - not filled at all?

4. Decision: If to fill, then proceed to job description and post-holder specification and advertisement.

Job description

This might well be either a specific description, a subject or department, say, History, or a generic job description such as head of year, or head of department, or head of faculty with the specific year or department written in.

It is helpful to divide the description into three parts:

1. the main responsibilities;

2. additional specific responsibilities;

3. general duties and responsibilities that are shared with other staff.

Under these three headings the following points should be addressed and set out:

Post title _____

Scale _____

Each of the outlines of responsibilities – the main responsibilities (1) and additional and specific responsibilities (2) should include the items listed below:

*   include to whom responsible;

*   responsibility for other staff;

*   responsibility for rooms, equipment, finance, etc;

*   responsibility for pupils;

*   training and staff development;

*   other relevant details;

*   pastoral duties;

*   administrative duties;

*   supervisory duties (general).

General duties and responsibilities (3) should appear in each job specification and outline there those matters which are the responsibilities of all staff.

Post-holder specification

1. Experience sought:
   - type of school;
   - age of pupils;
   - length of teaching experience.

2. Qualifications:
   - specific subject/academic;
   - general;
   - phase;
   - INSET updating.

3. Skills/Knowledge:
   - listed as required.

Advertisement

Consider:

1. Content – short and to the point, asking prospective candidates to send for further details.

2. Style.

3. Return **to** by **closing date**.

4. Materials to be sent to applicants
   - job specification
   - post-holder specification
   - information on school
     - size
     - ethos expectation
     - aims and objectives
     - organisation

Shortlisting

Who does this? It is good practice for it to be done by the head with an appointing group. How many candidates would you ideally commit to interview? The cost of that? Are you going to have a long list and reduce to a short list after seeking referees, or will you go directly to a short list for interview? Take in to account local practices or policies on use of references (open or confidential).

Criteria

You have already established these by the job and post-holder specification. Which candidates best match those?

References

Are you going to send a non-specific request or ask specific agreed questions? Enclose specification. Is the practice in your area to send for references after selection or to use open references only?

Invite candidates

- Give details of date, time, place.
- Give details of the arrangements for the interview.
- Give directions to location for interview.
- Give indication of expenses covered.

Arrangement for interview

1. Preparation
   - Think about questions to be asked. Who asks? Who interviews?
   - Are other techniques to be used? eg
     - intrays
     - analysis of a school problem
     - taking staff meeting
     - simulations, etc.

2. Schedule of visits and appointment with projected timings:
   - candidates see school;
   - meet head/deputies, relevant staff;
   - time of interview, and/or exercises.

3. Physical setting:
   - choice of room;
   - arrangement of room for candidates' interviews;
   - type of facilities used.

4. Interviews/Exercises:
   - creation of atmosphere that puts candidate at ease;

- procedure to be established;
- papers/summaries of candidates' details to interviewing panel;
- briefing of interview panel on task – refer to specification and criteria;
- establish questions to be asked so that each candidate is treated similarly (see below).

Interview questions

1. Maintain a balance between types of question – open, closed, multiple, hypothetical, those requiring self-assessment.

2. Questions to be in a logical order.

3. Discuss the nature and extent of supplementary follow-up questions.

4. Remind panel that questions relative to gender, race, religion, political or trade union affiliation, or of a personal family nature are not permitted and could lead to litigation or process in one form or another.

Decision

1. Discussion of each criterion.

2. Systematic discussion of each candidate from persons who are directly involved in the process.

3. Selection of one candidate who matches best the criteria.

4. Successful candidate told – who tells the unsuccessful?

5. Do you arrange a de-briefing for the unsuccessful?

Confirmation of verbal offer of post in writing

1. Letter to candidate – post, salary, start date, confirmation of job specification.

2. Letter to LEA giving photocopy or original of application form together with any accompanying letter of application and any disclosure of spent/unspent convictions.

Summary and further considerations

The establishment of policies, procedures and processes that are known and understood by the existing staff of the school and by external candidates provides the firmest foundation for making good effective appointments to the staff of the school, primarily because the principles, concepts and thought-processes are embodied in the procedures.

The additional bonus is that the danger of falling foul of any complaint under the sex/race, equal opportunities legislation and of any grievance on pay or promotion will have been significantly lessened, if not completely prevented. Certainly such complaints and grievances can be more completely answered if the procedures are fully completed. Each stage can be evidenced by the record made at the time.

Even more positively, good, accurate procedures that select effectively are cost effective, in spite of the need for thoroughness and hence expenditure of time, as 75–85 per cent of school budgets are expended on staffing.

Staffing: Pay and Conditions

Malcolm Hewitt

The 1991 Pay and Conditions Document charged 'Relevant Bodies' with the task of formulating and keeping under regular review a salary policy for the teachers in their schools. Here I attempt to give some guidance as to how that may be achieved, based on the assumption that the school in question has a fully delegated budget so that the 'Relevant Body' is the governing body. Inevitably, therefore, the role of the governors is central to the whole issue, particularly their attitude towards the pay flexibilities now available. While it is clear that in many cases there is either a 'won't pay' or a 'can't pay' attitude, nevertheless I suggest here how senior management teams, with their governors, might proceed.

This issue needs to be set in the context of three other important issues: first, LMS, which will play the major part in determining just how much flexibility really exists; second, the new Independent Review Body and its possible support for some form of performance related pay; and third, the importance of governor training – a responsibility of both the LEAs and senior management teams.

There are four very important sources of information which are critical in the process of forming a pay policy for your school (see Table 3.3.1). The 1991 Document is the legal basis for any decisions made by the governors and the Circular is the DES's interpretation of what the law says. The Statutory Instrument is crucial in determining how governor sub-committees are set up, and there are two important points that need to be emphasised in this connection.

1. The 1991 Pay and Conditions Document (and succeeding documents).

2. The supporting Circular 10/91.

3. The Statutory Instrument 1989 No 1503.

4. A suitable commentary is *Managing Procedures and Pay* by Brian Unwin and John Weeks, available at £6.50 from the Secondary Heads' Association, 130 Regent Road, Leicester LE1 7PG.

Table 3.3.1 *Sources of information on pay policy*

1. It will be impossible to work without a sub-committee structure for the simple reason that if the whole governing body makes decisions on these matters and an appeal is lodged by an aggrieved member of staff it will not be possible for the appeal to be heard.

2. It is essential that the sub-committee is legally constituted. This involves the decision to set up the sub-committee being made at a full governors' meeting when at least 75 per cent of the total possible number of governors is present.

Assuming, therefore, that a staffing committee has been legally constituted what follows is an outline pay policy in which I suggest various ways in which you might proceed and which incorporates all the issues above.

A typical pay policy will be a concise document and will include reference to the following:

1. The governors' role as good employers.

2. An emphasis on a whole school approach.

3. Equal opportunities and equal pay issues.

4. The remit of the staffing committee, and the right of appeal.

5. The use of the flexibilities.

6. An advertising policy.

The resulting policy should be published to all staff (Paragraph 34 of the Circular).

Paperbound! . . .

Wire-O® bound.

Discover the world of Wire-O® binding and transform all your paperwork into stylish and professionally presented documents.

For further details about our full range of desk top binding equipment, please contact Angela Pullen at James Burn International.

PB3000

PB34

EcATT *programme* **Delivering Economic and Industrial Understanding in the National Curriculum**

Having trouble with any of the following ...

* Clarifying the links between Economic and Industrial Understanding and National Curriculum programmes of study and attainment targets?
* Planning a development programme for EIU?
* Implementing EIU in subject areas?
* Planning and meeting staff training needs?
* Developing the economic dimension of the work related curriculum?

EcATT offers...

* a consultancy and evaluation service to help individual schools, colleges, LEAs, TECs and EBPs
* a programme of one, two and five day short courses for coordinators & teachers
* accreditation at M.A., M.Ed. and Diploma levels
* access to a national network of curriculum development activities and resources
* regular workshops for education advisers

Give EcATT a call at..

Institute of Education **or**	School of Education **or**	Department of Education
University of London	University of Manchester	University College of Swansea
Tel.071 612 6445	Tel. 061 273 4452	Tel. 0792 201231 Ext.2028

An Outline Pay Policy

There should be an opening statement of intent. For example:

> The 1991 Teachers' Pay and Conditions of Service Document charged governing bodies with devising pay policies to take account of the flexibilities available within a national framework. This governing body wishes to be seen as a good employer concerned with many resource issues – buildings, equipment, INSET, career development, etc – as well as with recruiting, retaining and motivating its teachers and non-teaching staff. This document is only part of that exercise and deals in the main with a pay policy for the school's teachers.
>
> The implementation of the policy will be the responsibility of the staffing committee, the details of which are given below.

The committee will take into account in all decisions involving promotions, affordability, equal opportunities and equal pay issues.

Staffing committee

This section should contain the names of its members. A committee of four, five or six is suggested, plus the headteacher whether or not he/she is a governor.

Remit

This should be a simple statement of those areas the committee will cover. The committee's main purpose is to formulate and regularly review the salary policy for the staff. Other areas will include: staffing levels; the number and structure of incentive allowances; establishing criteria for the use of all discretionary elements described in the Document; an annual review of the salaries of all staff on 1 September; and an advertising and appointments system. There should also be a statement that this committee will be responsible for other issues such as discipline, dismissal and a regular review and appraisal procedure. Finally, this section should contain the names of the appeal committee.

Pay flexibilities

There is a need, I believe, before embarking on the implementation of a pay policy to consider the base point. In other words, it would be prudent to suggest a complete review of the salary of every teacher in the school including the head and deputies on a particular date – say 1 September in the financial year in which full LMS delegation is achieved. This review would look at the incentive allowance system as well as the spine position of the head and deputies. (The criteria to be used for reviewing the spine position of Heads and Deputies would be spelt out later in the policy.) In other words, what follows in the pay policy is then based upon an assumption that the starting point for all staff is correct.

Criteria

The appointment of new teachers to the profession

Good honours graduates will start at point 3 and other teachers and graduates at point 1. It is possible to move all new appointments to the school up by 2 points. There are, however, great dangers in so doing because of the effect on other teachers appointed earlier to whom this 'extra' was not awarded. However, you may consider the case of a teacher without a good honours degree but who has an outstanding Post Graduate Certificate of Education as worthy of consideration.

In addition you will need to state what you will do with new entrants who are aged 23 or over who have relevant experience, maybe in another field. It is possible to put such teachers at a point no higher than they would have reached if they had started at the age of 22.

The appointment of any teacher to the school

Most governors will see little use for the discretion to move new appointments two points up the scale. However, if the governors are clear that a post has become difficult to fill then its use may be considered, but a clear definition of 'difficult to fill' will be needed.

In the realm of market focus, governors may wish to use an enhancement or a discretionary scale point, say to the value of £549 for one year, as an inducement to join the school. Note here, that the DES is of the opinion that discretionary scale points *can* be offered to newly appointed staff.

Incremental progression

It will be normal for all teachers to move up one point on the scale each September until point 10 is reached. Care needs to be taken if the power to withhold such a point is used. Any teacher in this situation needs to be given every opportunity to put things right.

Teachers can also receive increments at any time during the year but, except in the case of a teacher achieving good honours graduate status, who would then be entitled to two increments, governors may see little use for this discretion.

Incremental enhancement

The governors may enhance the value of incremental points 1 to 9 by £273, £549, £822 or £1092 provided the next incremental point is not exceeded. There are numerous ways in which governors may consider using this discretion, for example:

- As an inducement to join the school, as mentioned above.

- For a specific short-term responsibility.

- As part of a performance-related package (see below).

It needs to be clearly understood that all such awards will be at most for one year only and in any event will have to be reviewed on 1 September every year irrespective of when they are awarded.

Incentive allowances

In general these are well understood and in spite of the criteria laid down (eg responsibility, outstanding classroom ability, shortage subjects or for a post difficult to fill) they are nearly always given for responsibility, as this is often seen as by far the most important criterion.

Read carefully Annexe A in the Document which sets out guidelines for the numbers of incentive allowances to be used. Remember only the minimum overall figure has statutory force.

Governors may wish to consider temporary allowances for short-to-medium-term specific responsibilities.

Discretionary scale points

This is the most difficult area, not least because it is likely to involve about 80 per cent of all teachers. There is only one criterion laid down: performance across all aspects of professional activity. As this is clearly a version of performance related pay, governors may wish to consider it in conjunction with incremental enhancement and create a scale of say, £272, £549, £822, £1092, £2000, £3000.

We need to be clear what is meant by 'all aspects of professional activity' and I suggest it can be thought of in four main areas:

1. Performance in the classroom.

2. Performance in other roles.

3. Contribution to development work.

4. Contribution to the wider aspects of school life.

There are many ways in which such awards could be made – private deals, heads' recommendations, equal shares, or by application and interview – but I believe great danger exists if the system is not seen to be open and fair to everyone. Indeed rewarding a few could have a major demoralising effect on the many. I suggest, therefore, that governors may wish specifically to consider every teachers' position regularly, say every four years, and make an award then on the evidence provided by the teacher concerned and the head. At least by this means, there is a strong element of fairness and affordability attached. The head could use all the information known to him/her, including knowledge of any appraisal statement (but not the statement itself).

Finally the governors will need to determine whether such an award is permanent or annual. The budget may only stand an annual award, except in the case of a teacher carrying a major responsibility under (4) above, for which an incentive allowance is inappropriate and when an award could be permanent.

Heads and deputies

Heads' and deputies' salaries are determined by referring to a 51-point spine. The relevant point on the spine will normally be within a range. The spine and the range of points are on pages 6 and 7 of the Document. Paragraph 51 of the Circular is crucial and the issues that need to be addressed are:

1. A minimum differential between any deputy and the next highest paid teacher – 12 per cent is a guide.

2. The relationship between the head and deputies' pay – 80 per cent is a guide.

3. The number of deputies. In Annexe A of the Document only the minimum has statutory force.

4. Whether the deputies should be paid at different rates.

In determining these issues, governors must have regard to the criteria laid down, ie, responsibility, posts difficult to fill, socio-economic status of the pupils' parents, and performance. I would add length of service. Governors should consider a system of regular review as suggested above for teachers, and further determine whether any increases should be annual, permanent or temporary. Note that if a temporary award is made, say of two spine points, for three years after that time the salary level would be reduced to the original spine point.

Advertising policy

Governors will need to determine whether all posts will, whenever possible, be filled following applications and interviews even if for internal candidates. In addition the policy should state the arrangements for interviewing panels for various levels of appointments – standard scale, allowances A, B, etc, and finally deputy head and headteacher.

This chapter has touched the surface of some of the problems surrounding the creation of a pay policy. My advice is: 'make haste slowly'. The governing body should make sure that the staff and unions have been consulted, that the governors have the information they need to understand the issues, and that the budget is not destroyed.

Managing Staff Development

Margaret Nicholls

Climate

Much of the best professional development appears to happen by osmosis. Of course this is not so, but where the management of a school has created a receptive climate, where the staff are involved in the planning and decision-making and where everyone, teaching and non-teaching staff alike, has access to quality training opportunities, then colleagues' enthusiasm and inspiration transmits itself to others and becomes a significant motivating factor.

The creation of this climate should not be left to chance. Clear perceptions of the importance of participation, of crisp organisation, of breadth and balance, will ensure staff commitment to the exercise which should be seen as a normal, integrated part of the professional, day-to-day life of the institution. The highest levels of performance can be observed where reviewing, recording and evaluating are seen as an integral part of any and every task. The motivation to reach the highest possible level is an intensely personal factor and not all colleagues will follow the same path or strive for the same ends but the ethos of the institution has a profound and very marked effect on the motivation of the personnel.

Motivation

The factors which motivate colleagues to become actively involved in planned professional development are many and varied. One may be seeking promotion, another may perceive a gap in his or her own personal performance, yet another may strive to emulate a colleague or a friend. Frequently the perceptions are linked to either self-assessment or professional appreciation, often of a more senior colleague.

Appraisal, sensitively handled and imaginatively organised, may also be a key motivating factor.

The creation of open working groups, either within departments or faculties or across the whole staff, where colleagues feel at ease and confident, with a clear working brief, will go much of the way towards identifying needs and key areas both for individuals and for groups, and to stimulating commitment.

Access

It would be interesting to set up a format for staff development from scratch but few management teams enjoy that luxury. Most start from where they are at and there will be significant differences in levels of expectation and in ranges of experience. Access is an all-important factor and is difficult to separate from the concept of climate.

It is essential to designate key personnel and to ensure that all colleagues appreciate the roles of these people. For example, many staff expect, and all should demand, right of access to the head for personal, private consultations on their own professional progress. After all, who writes the references for promotion? Who has easy access to the corridors of power within LEAs and their inspectorates? Some colleagues may be wary initially of broaching the subject of personal progression directly with the head. In the best run institutions heads of department, heads of year/house, or heads of faculties have written into their job descriptions responsibility for initiating professional development within their own staff teams.

Many institutions have a formal group headed by a senior member of staff which takes responsibility for the day-to-day running of in-service training, planning and information sharing. The most successful of these function as consultative groups for the entire staff. Membership is open, debate is free but within established structures, and colleagues generally feel they have access to information and acceptance in the planning cycles.

Organisation

There are many possible models of organisation but all have common factors – how/when/where/who? – and if we wish to be successful we ignore these at our peril.

Using questionnaires

Initially, it is helpful to have an analysis of what colleagues' perceptions are of their own needs, of their own priorities and their own capacity. Key staff (eg assistant teacher, head of department, head of year/house, senior teacher, deputy head, administrative colleague) can profitably work together to assist the whole staff in developing a questionnaire or a review sheet which the in-service group can then analyse before beginning to plan a year's in-service programme.

Balance needs

Alongside this, it is essential to review the aims and objectives of the institution to enable the management of the school to prioritise the needs which will inevitably be expressed. A balance has to be maintained between providing in-service training opportunities which are essential to benefit the students and those which will of necessity have a personal reward for individual members of staff.

Use existing resources

In addition, it is useful to review what potential there is within the institution for providing expertise, what may be on offer within the LEA, (teachers' centres, advisory/inspectorate staff, specialist teams, etc.) and what colleagues from other institutions may also be able to offer.

Those responsible for the school's budget, and particularly the professional development section of that budget, will appreciate local resources being tapped before they begin to look at outside consultancies.

Using information

Finally information processing systems are vital to the success of any professional development programme. Currently schools are circulated with offers of training opportunities. These need sifting, categorising and displaying. Consultation early on between the institution's timetabling team and the professional development/in-service group may enable blocks of time to be organised within non-contact arrangements, which can be classified as potential training/development slots, thereby enabling appropriate groups of staff to work together and avoiding unnecessary disruption to the teaching timetable.

Feedback and review

There needs to be a forum for reviewing who should go on what courses and how dissemination of the information and insight gained may be achieved on return. Naturally this needs to be linked to the information already culled about priorities, school and personal needs. It is then essential that someone within the institution (and preferably more than just the head) has an overview of the whole pattern.

This implies tight organisation, good record-keeping and easy access for all involved.

Finance

Budgetary considerations have a vital part to play in ensuring that staff are satisfied with any proposals for professional development. With the advent of LMS more open access to school financial policies often brings added advantages. Value for money has to be demonstrated. How else can expenditure be justified? It is the clear responsibility of the head together with the governors, in reviewing the allocation of resources, to set aside an appropriate sum to be devoted exclusively to in-service training/professional development. The whole staff should be aware of the mechanics of this exercise even if the responsibility and accountability is then lodged with the appropriate working group. Given the fact that training opportunities rarely arrive regularly and neither does staff demand, the more flexible a budget can be, the better. It is essential that those responsible for allocating resources retain a contingency fund to enable them to seize opportunities as and when they present themselves.

Sponsorship

There is rarely sufficient money to cover every eventuality. When planning training sessions which are either institution-led or - based, it is well worth investigating sponsorship in one form or another, for example from local hotels and catering organisations for venues and provisions, from local industry and commerce for expertise, facilities and consumable resources. Educational charities too are often a source of funds, particularly for individual professional development sponsorship.

It is well worth the investment of one person's time within the in-service group, the finance group, or the school as a whole, to check out all the possible alternative sources of finance.

Prime considerations

Finally, what are the most important issues to address when considering professional development for colleagues? Surely the most important has to be adequate provision, followed by right of access. Every colleague from the newest probationer to the most senior member of staff heading for retirement is entitled to support and development at whatever level he or she feels is appropriate at the time.

Information and communication throughout the institution are vital. Institutions that flourish in all areas are those where equal support is given to their non-tutorial staff. The quality of response given by dining-room assistants, by caretaking and services staff, not to mention administrative, secretarial and technician staff, is mirrored by quality provision for the students.

Proper participative planning and whole-school review and evaluation will enable everyone to feel that their professional development opportunities are one of the most valuable features of their professional lives.

KEY ISSUES

- Establish the needs of *all* staff.

- Ensure ownership by wide consultation.

- Embed the policy in the school development plan.

- Ensure sensitive handling of non-teaching staff and provide relevant, appropriate agendas carefully linked to whole school policy.

- Evaluate information and communication systems and adjust as appropriate.

References

1 Brighouse, T., *What Makes a Good School?* Teaching and Learning Series, Network Educational Press,

2 Donnelly, J., (1991) Secondary Heads' Association, 130 Regent Road, Leicester LE1 7PG. (£3.50). *Managing Inset*,

3 *The Staff Development Manual*, Framework Press.

The Educated Choice

The Group Viewer is the ultimate schoolproof television and video facility specially developed for schools, universities and colleges. Rigorously conforming to the tilt, stability and robustness safety requirements in BS4958, the Group Viewer is the safest product available. It can be built up to meet your specifications and budget requirements by choosing from a range of televisions and videos.

In addition to the Group Viewer, we can also provide a comprehensive range of television, video and related products. These include professional satellite systems, distribution networks, interactive workstations and courseware, public address systems, small screen televisions, play-only videos and camcorders.

And, as part of THORN EMI plc, we have the national resources to provide a comprehensive local service, including delivery, installation and maintenance.

For further information and details of our financing options, including purchase, lease or rental, please call 0628 822181.

◢◣ THORN EMI Business Communications

Highfield House, Foundation Park, 8 Roxborough Way, Maidenhead, Berkshire SL6 3TZ.

Using Video for Professional Development

Maurice Plaskow

Information is the raw material from which knowledge is manufactured. The process requires a range of skills; the result should be understanding.

Information on its own produces only as much understanding as copying pages from a reference book. This is no more an educational activity than is a belief that simply reading articles on or guides to the current initiatives – whether LMS, technology, the national curriculum, school management – will automatically lead to their effective implementation.

LMS is *really* about setting priorities, and relating these to the school development plan. Only then can one sensibly allocate appropriate resources. Most other things flow from this process. Teacher appraisal is not so much about accountability as professional development, in order to enhance performance, with the main aim of achieving more effective learning on the part of the students.

INSET

All these activities require some form of training: a marrying of experience with new insights. Teachers have always recognised the need for professional updating. In the past this has most often been sought through courses or conferences. These did not, however, ensure a sharing of the new-found expertise, or a necessary application to particular circumstances. The growth of school-based INSET (in-service education for teachers) programmes is much more likely to meet the needs of individual schools and their staffs – not forgetting ancillary and support staff as well as teachers.

Many schools have appointed INSET coordinators to undertake a needs analysis followed by a planned, coherent programme in consultation with colleagues. However, it is one thing to identify needs; quite another to decide how they can best be met.

The increasing range of provision

Probably the first reaction is to look for the 'expert': someone who will dispense a prescription, if not wisdom. But within any group of staff there are already experts on a wide range of issues – many of them unrecognised. Some of the most valuable INSET sessions are given by teachers to their own colleagues, with far greater credibility, and considerably less cost.

Books and articles are still the most readily accessible and flexible pieces of technology. They do, however, need to be read and analysed. Although schools have for many years used television in the classroom for curriculum purposes, they have not made systematic use of the medium for their own education and training. Video is a good way to capture events and help people inside an experience. Although any observer to an event will slightly change its nature, video is the nearest we can yet achieve to authenticity. It has several added advantages:

- it is a familiar medium which, through broadcasting, brings authority to content;

- it is marvellously flexible: it can be stopped, restarted, replayed, and will never lose patience with the viewers;

- it can raise issues in a dramatic and succinct form;

- it can show sequences of processes and illuminate them with commentary and graphics;

- it can 'distance' sensitive and controversial issues, and help objective analysis;

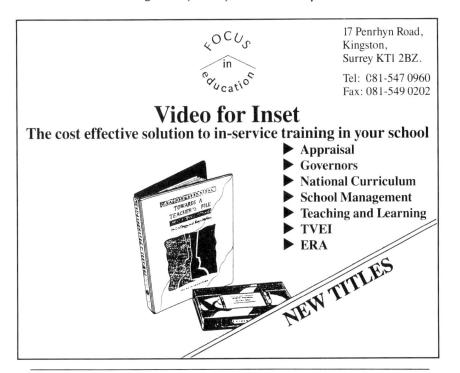

- it is very cost-effective;

- it can be used by individuals and groups for study and discussion;

- it provides a shared experience and a common starting point for exploration.

The DES has itself commissioned a number of training packages, particularly for school and college governors, and there are many other sources of material which can provide the core for training sessions on a wide variety of topics of current interest. What has to be recognised is that many of these videos are not 'programmes' in the conventional broadcast sense: they are not meant to be viewed at a single sitting from beginning to end. Indeed, this will often destroy their usefulness, which lies in close study of short episodes. Three or four minutes of video can easily sustain an entire session of one or two hours if linked with discussion and simulation exercises as well as individual and group tasks related to what has been seen.

Much of what is shown is not presented as a model; rather an example. This should encourage viewers to examine their own practice, compare structures and procedures within their own institutions, and share perceptions with colleagues.

Part Four

Curriculum Management

4.1

Managing The Curriculum

Barry Hilditch

Managing the curriculum in the early 1990s includes the added responsibility of implementing the National Curriculum and adapting to the shift of control of governing bodies as a result of the 1988 Education Reform Act. Both these represent a significant change from the historical situation in which individual schools had almost complete autonomy over the curriculum and what was taught in the classroom. The change is an enforced one and one which will present curriculum managers with a new challenge: delivering a prescribed set of subjects and having the effectiveness of that delivery monitored and judged more than ever before.

Who controls the curriculum?

It is essential that all groups involved in the planning and organisation of a school recognise who controls the nature and shape of the curriculum. The responsibilities of the governing body and the headteacher are set out in Table 4.1.1.

The headteacher

To fulfil his or her responsibilities in planning and managing the curriculum, the headteacher should:

Governing Body	Headteacher
Decides curriculum policy (including sex education and RE)	Proposes a detailed curriculum plan which ensures delivery of statutory elements
Confirms the delivery of the curriculum; receives reports	Organises the delivery of the curriculum; monitors and reports
Decides number of staff required to deliver the curriculum	Advises on number and skills of staff needed

Table 4.1.1   *Division of responsibilities for the curriculum*

- involve, and join in discussion with, the teaching staff;

- in consultation with senior colleagues, present the governing body with the views of school staff;

- work with the governors to produce and agree the curriculum;

- after consultation, produce the curricular aspects of the school development plan, which indicates the nature of the curriculum for the next two to three years.

The governing body

It is the duty of the governors to take account of:

- The National Curriculum both as expressed in traditional subject headings and as cross-curricular themes;

- the LEA Curriculum Policy Statement;

- TVEI curriculum requirements, if appropriate;

- the school and its own views and policies;

- the requirements of parents and the wider community;

- equal opportunities;

- continuity from key stage 2 of the curriculum, from associated primary schools.

School management

The senior management team within the school has a key role to play in curriculum planning and development. Working with the governors, it advises them on legislation and puts before them the views of other concerned bodies. Once the governors have decided on the curriculum, the team ensures its implementation and checks that it is delivered effectively. It also has to ensure that under LMS, proposed changes (including staffing) can be financed from the school budget.

Finally the senior management team establishes a calendar which allows for periods of consultation and the appropriate timescale for change. Time needed for some changes, such as the timing of the school day, is laid down in statute.

Middle management within the school (usually heads of department and/or faculty) is responsible for delivering the *content* of the curriculum. Their role must now change, as they take account of the detailed guidelines of the National Curriculum. The flair and imagination of the best teachers will now need to be concentrated on effective delivery within the classroom and not on deciding which areas of a subject are to be selected. Any proposed changes in syllabuses should ideally in future be notified to senior management for approval, as the head has statutory duties to ensure the delivery of the approved curriculum.

Key questions to be addressed

There are several key questions which need to be addressed at school level. These include:

Timing and organisation of the school day

Is the present timing and format of the day/week the best for the effective delivery of the curriculum? DES circular 7/90, Management of the School Day, recommended that pupils aged 12 to 16 should receive 24 hours a week of instruction. (This does not have legal force.) As a result of this, and the demands of the National Curriculum, the 40-period week seems to be disappearing, with 25 one-hour lessons becoming popular, especially when linked to

maximising teaching time in the morning. Assemblies are often now being held at the beginning or end of the afternoon session.

Balance of time

It is important to note that the balance of time for individual subjects can be managed over the length of the key stage; in other words, they do not have to be equalised for every year. For example, a school may decide that Mathematics, Science and English should have an equal amount of time for key stage 3 but this can only be achieved over three years (see box).

Year	Mathematics	Science	English
7	3	3	4
8	4	3	3
9	3	4	3

Course time

It may be worth looking at the length of time required to deliver the different types of course. In a school year of 190 days, not all are effectively used to deliver the curriculum. It is more realistic to take 185 days and multiply them by the number of teaching hours in a day, to give an approximate total of the number of hours available for the whole curriculum.

If the day has a nominal five hours, then 925 hours are available. Key stage 3 therefore has 2775 hours. Key stage 4 is not, however, 1850 hours, as the number of days in year 11 is reduced by at least the examination period.

It may be helpful to ask the heads of subject to calculate the number of hours they need to deliver the curriculum demands for each key stage. The answers will be varied, interesting and almost certainly will add up to more than the time available! The nature and requirements of key stage 4 courses – long and short ones – add even more interest to this question.

The National Curriculum

The early stages, pre-1992, of implementing key stage 3 into the 11 to 16 curriculum will not have presented many problems for the majority of schools.

	Key Stage 3			Key Stage 4	
	7	8	9	10	11
English	*	*	*	*	
Science	*	*	*	*	
Mathematics	*	*	*	*	
Technology	*	*	*		
Geography	*	*			
History	*	*			
Modern Language	*				
Art	*				
Music	*				
PE	*				
Welsh				* (dates can vary)	
* implemented in year group in 1992					

Table 4.1.2 *National Curriculum checklist, September 1992*

September 1992 represents an interesting and important stage in the implementation of the National Curriculum, with the first year of key stage 3 being fully in place. Schools may still be fine-tuning their plans for years 8 and 9, while still wrestling with the difficulties of key stage 4. Table 4.1.2 sets out a checklist for September 1992 of where schools will be.

Subject decisions

Different subjects are at different stages of implementation.

Science: policy decisions should have been made by now.

Geography and History: final discussions should be taking place on key stage 4 for 1994 implementation; this could be a choice between the subjects or to do a short course in both.

Modern Language: the exact nature of languages in key stage 4 is now under discussion. One particular point to be decided is whether pupils should experience more than one foreign language.

The Arts: with the implementation of Art and Music in year 7, a policy decision for key stage 3 should be in place: will it be separate subjects or is it being delivered through an expressive or performing arts course? At key stage 4 one has to decide whether the Arts are to be offered at all. If so, are they to be separate subjects or a combined course, possibly for all pupils? Combined courses can be offered as the Arts are not a required part of the National Curriculum at key stage 4.

PE: the pressures of fitting in the National Curriculum should not be solved by cutting back PE.

Other subjects: the number of non-National Curriculum subjects to be offered will depend upon the size of the school, whether or not it has a 6th form, and what local demands are. There should, however, be a critical look at what the whole curriculum offers to the individual pupil.

Cross-curricular themes: these are easily forgotten but play an important part in retaining the breadth and balance of the curriculum. This applies even more so to Personal and Social Education, which, in my view, should be preserved and not squeezed out under the pressure of parental demands for even more examination subjects.

The above is designed to act as a reminder for curriculum planners and as a checklist for those managing the curriculum for the first time. Each school will arrive at its own solution but it will be interesting to see how schools face up to the challenge of a nationally prescribed curriculum.

Part Five

Marketing and Sponsorship

PLUG INTO LUCOZADE ENERGY

Now you can offer your customers a healt refreshing change of soft drinks from the r **Lucozade** vending machine.

At the touch of a button your custom can choose:

Lucozade – No. 1 glucose energy drink.

***Lucozade* *SPORT* – No. 1 isotonic sports drink.**

Sparkling Ribena – No. 1 carbonated blackcurr flavour vitamin C drink.

We put a great deal of energy into keer these brands out in front and we spend a mas £20 million annually on TV, cinema, press poster support.

So plug into **Lucozade** vending and sw on to this new source of profit, today.

SB SmithKline Beecham

SmithKline Beecham Consumer Brands,
Department V, SB House, Great West Road, Brentford, Middx. TW8 9BD.

Marketing and Public Relations for Schools

Laurence French

What is marketing about?

The legislation of 1988 has created a completely different climate for schools to operate in, allowing them to shape their own development to a degree previously enjoyed only by those in the private sector. State schools are now able to determine their own priorities, allocate funding from a budget and market themselves. It is this term 'market' that is for many among the new and possibly daunting exercises that educational managers have to carry out, conjuring up images of slick advertising packages or free giveaways to sell the virtues of a particular school. I hope that it will become apparent that marketing is in fact none of these things, and that schools that decide to go ahead with a marketing policy might well be simply formalising and structuring those things they already do to 'sell themselves'. Marketing provides a more professional approach, bringing into sharper focus a range of strategies already employed, and under LMS perhaps allowing schools to budget for them and extend their scope.

What then is 'marketing'? The Institute of Marketing defines it as 'the management process of identifying, anticipating and satisfying customer requirements profitably'. The word 'profitably' clearly differentiates business marketing from that of a school. However,

the rest of the definition can stand as a model for what we are about. Marketing is a management skill of identifying what our 'customers' (or perhaps more accurately, the stakeholders of a school) want from us as educationalists, and of satisfying those needs as best we can under the financial and practical constraints within which we operate. It is a process of gearing the school to the customer, of understanding the customer so well that the 'product' sells itself. Marketing is about public relations and PR is the celebration of good performance, as well as recognising the need to improve poor performance. The process of communication is paramount here and is at the heart of all good PR and marketing.

Much of what we consider to be PR or marketing is done within the actual institution; in fact about 70 per cent of marketing is an internal procedure, with the other 30 per cent directed outwards toward the public. For a school deciding on how to market itself, this provides a useful starting point. Look at yourself first, then worry about the outside world!

Why market your school?

Careful and wise marketing can have a number of benefits for the school. It can, for example, give you a far greater understanding of your mission – your strengths and weaknesses. It can create a corporate identity and feeling of pride among the staff and pupils; it can help unite the various interest groups that inevitably arise within such complex institutions; and it can show the public – often misinformed about education – what real progress and developments have taken place in your school. It will, one hopes, attract more people (and therefore pupils) to come to see your school, putting it in the public eye so that parents can make choices based on knowledge rather than hearsay. It can attract much-needed funds or equipment, and help to satisfy the needs and aspirations of pupils and parents. It can ask some fundamental and searching questions about the school to show you a way forward.

An outline strategy

The question now arises – where do you start? The following is not a definitive scheme by any means, but it is a possible series of

strategies and decisions that provide a systematic framework for marketing and public relations.

1. Establish a marketing planning group
    Communication is at the heart of all good PR and marketing. Within your staff there is a wealth of untapped talent – writers, artists, designers, communicators. Remember, though, that the process must be management-driven and a senior member of staff should ideally co-ordinate policy. Keep all staff informed as often as possible.

2. Set realistic targets
    Avoid the trap of trying to do too much too soon. Start with easily attainable targets, if possible those that will give you fairly rapid success. This tends to win over the sceptics quicker than anything else.

3. Do a SWOT analysis
    Having decided to go ahead, with the market planning group formed, you will need to examine your school carefully and honestly to find out what needs doing. SWOT analysis (see

below) provides a framework for such an analysis.

Strengths – What are the strengths of your school? How can you capitalise on them? What are the unique selling points (USPs)? Remember strengths can be perceived by some as weaknesses too.

Weaknesses – Be as honest as you can here. All schools have them. Are they the sort of weaknesses that can be improved? Are they beyond your control?

Opportunities – What opportunities are coming up as good PR and marketing material in the long and short term (concerts, trips, new courses)?

Threats – Accepting the fact that some might be beyond your control, keep tabs on the environment, problems and developments. Read the local press to get an overview of the situation. Find out what other schools are planning (opting out, for example).

4. Identify your markets

Inside the school – without the backing of the head, the understanding and support of governors and the goodwill of colleagues, your planning group will not get far. Keep people informed. Let them become part of the process too. Don't forget that your greatest and most numerous ambassadors are the pupils – use them, tell them what is happening, get their support. A badge or logo on a blazer or sweatshirt is a potent mobile advertising tool.

Outside the school – consider the importance of the following stakeholders in your school's development and marketing plan: parents, local businesses, voluntary organisations, past pupils, the local community, LEA personnel, inspectors and advisers, student teachers, visitors from other schools, colleges or universities, partner-school teachers, parents and pupils – in fact, anyone who comes into contact with your school on a regular or casual basis, professional or non-professional.

5. Ways of promoting the school
   Give thought to how the following will benefit your marketing strategy:

   - use of the media (local and national press, radio and TV)

- production of brochures, prospectuses (now a legal requirement), promotional videos.
- marketing and PR potential of exhibitions, open days, sports events, parents' evenings (or days?), special events held at school outside normal working hours (particularly applicable for community schools).
- format and style of all written communications to parents and other interested stakeholders.
- links with industry or non-commercial organisations, Chamber of Commerce, FE/HE institutions.
- contacts with community leaders.

Internal marketing

It has already been established that about 70 per cent of your marketing will be done 'in-house'. A good starting point is to look at yourself through the eyes of a visitor (a new parent or a prospective member of staff perhaps?). Start at the gate and take a good look at the place.

- Are the signposts clear?

- Is the way to reception obvious for the first-time visitor?

- Does the place look inviting or is there yesterday's or even last week's litter still blowing around? (It is surprising what you get used to and are prepared to overlook when working in a school.)

Move to the reception area.

- Is it warm and comfortable?

- How efficient are your office staff in welcoming visitors?

- What about the decor?

- Is there anywhere that says 'Welcome to . . . school?

Once you start looking for these sorts of details, it will soon become clear what needs to be done to improve that all-important first impression.

Some of these concerns can be dealt with very quickly and easily and improvements will be seen and appreciated by those using the school. People will begin to show greater interest in the way the school looks and might volunteer their services or suggestions. You are now beginning to involve others and they are beginning to see that marketing is not the anathema they once considered it to be.

In my own school we set up small working groups to look at and report on a number of areas: the buildings, the site, furniture, etc; another group looked at the school publications and how they could be improved; one concerned itself with curriculum matters (the product we sell); another with how the school was represented in the press.

As soon as you start asking yourself some fundamental questions (remember the SWOT analysis?), others will be generated and you can deal with them as and when you feel the need or have the resources. You will be surprised how soon the interest grows when your colleagues realise that what you are doing is helping to secure their future as well as that of the pupils and the school.

Other internal marketing strategies may well require more planning and thought. Poor examination performance or perceived poor discipline, for example, can have an adverse effect on your long-term marketing plans, particularly in these competitive days with open enrolment and greater parent power. These are not going to be remedied overnight. However, by showing your publics (parents, pupils, LEA etc) that attempts are being made to improve these aspects, and by involving your major stakeholders in the process, you are not only demonstrating a willingness to communicate your concerns to others, but showing that changes and innovations will be made – a PR success out of what might have seemed a lost cause.

Communication – the heart of the matter

At the beginning of this chapter I stated that good communications are central to effective PR and marketing. A word first about verbal communication. In his book *Thriving on Chaos*, American management consultant Tom Peters devoted a whole chapter to marketing by word of mouth. In it he says:

> Word of mouth is governed by the 90–10 rule: 90 per cent of the world is influenced by the other 10 per cent ... Every person who is interviewed, or delivers a package or visits a company walks away with an impression. If the company employees communicate effectively,

BRING A BREATH OF FRESH AIR INTO THE CLASSROOM
with Johnstone's Paints

Tough, durable, clean and safe - Johnstone's Paints' environmentally user friendly products are the ideal answer for the classroom.

Johnstone's Paints Water Based Gloss System and Acrylic Eggshell Finish are quick and easy to apply on internal surfaces and have virtually no odour. Both these products get top marks for cutting labour costs in half.

And it doesn't just end there! For exteriors, Johnstone's Paints manufacture a wide range of masonry coatings - so whether it's a question of cost, quality, colour or coating, Johnstone's Paints will do the homework for you.

Plus! They offer a whole range of FREE services to aid you in your decision making:

● **Specification Team.**
Johnstone's Paints team of Specification Advisors will liaise with yourselves or your contractors to ensure you get the right products at the right price.

● **Colour Advisory Service.**
This service can produce design and colour schemes for you - all presented in a professional, easy to understand manner.

● **Technical Back-up Service.**
Available from all Johnstone's Paints Branches it will enable you to achieve the most satisfactory and cost effective solution to any decorating problem.

● **Extensive Product Range.**
Johnstone's manufacture a wide range of products to tackle any job - including special coatings to provide the answer to difficult problems.

● **Nationwide Branch Network.**
With branches throughout the UK, Johnstone's Paints offer a Free, 24 hour delivery service, with no minimum order quantity.

Step up with **JOHNSTONE'S PAINTS**

The Professional Name for Quality

HEAD OFFICE AND FACTORY
Stonebridge House, Edge Lane, Droylsden, Manchester M35 6BX.
Tel: 061 370 7525 Fax: 061 370 0180

BIRMINGHAM TEL: 021 558 7761
BOLTON TEL: 0204 26049
BRADFORD TEL: 0274 370841
BRIGHTON TEL: 0273 204222
BRISTOL TEL: 0272 779251
CARDIFF TEL: 0222 344114
DERBY TEL: 0332 296622

EDINBURGH TEL: 031 553 5350
GLASGOW TEL: 041 429 8585
HANLEY TEL: 0782 214889
HULL TEL: 0482 27633
LEEDS TEL: 0532 445313
LEICESTER TEL: 0533 531119
LIVERPOOL TEL: 051 207 2921

LONDON (BOW) TEL: 081 980 3663
LONDON (CROYDON) TEL: 081 654 3192
LONDON (GREENFORD) TEL: 081 575 1604
MANCHESTER TEL: 061 872 4644
MIDDLESBROUGH TEL: 0642 243636
NOTTINGHAM TEL: 0602 580196
PRESTON TEL: 0772 556721

READING TEL: 0734 755886
SHEFFIELD TEL: 0742 730361
SOUTHAMPTON TEL: 0703 233100
WALSALL TEL: 0922 615131

COLOUR ADVISORY SERVICE
TEL: 0204 20472

every person who comes in contact with the company becomes a salesperson for the company, a carrier of goodwill about the company.

A casual derogatory (albeit jokey) remark over a drink or on the golf course can undo years of hard work; an over-worked and perhaps therefore over-officious secretary on the phone can create entirely the wrong impression; background chatter in the staff room while the phone is off the hook can do the same. There are all sorts of little traps out there waiting for you. To paraphrase the US airforce 'the price of good marketing is eternal vigilance'.

Written materials will form a large part of your communications and a vital link in your marketing policy. These not only affect how your school appears to others (the poorly typed letter to parents, for example) but influence whether the messages are clear to the non-professional. Consider your stakeholders. These are important people in the life of your school and should be treated with respect. Part of the way of showing respect is presenting them with information that *they* need in a way that shows *you* care.

The checklist in Table 5.1.1 might be useful when considering the format and style of your publications.

- Is everything written on A4? Could other size paper be used to add variety? Colour coding?

- Could you use a Desk Top Publishing (DTP) facility?

- Do all letters, brochures and so on follow a standard format?

- Have you an easily recognisable logo or letterhead?

- What is your house style/colour? Do you have one?

- Do you or can you include illustrations or photographs?

- How can you liven up otherwise 'dry' material?

- Have you seen what your competitors are producing?

- Does the same person always write the material, eg the head? What about other members of staff or pupils?

Table 5.1.1 *A checklist for your publications*

Media relations

The press

Much of your public relations will involve dealings with the press. To maximise the potential you need to know the best way of handling the press and appreciate the constraints under which they work. The *Press Release* is the best and most professional way of getting information to the newspapers. The conventions that should be observed when preparing one are shown in Table 5.1.2.

- The document should always be typed or word-processed on headed paper.
- The words PRESS RELEASE should be clearly written across the top.
- Remember to put on the date and reference number.
- Text should be double spaced with wide margins.
- Try to use a catchy headline.
- Text should contain the WHO, WHAT, WHERE, WHEN, WHY and HOW of the story.
- Include a quote from a person connected with the text.
- Use one side only of A4 and no more than two sheets.
- End press release by the word ENDS, two or three times across the bottom of the page.
- Include the name and phone number of contact person. A home number is always appreciated as journalists rarely work office hours, or they may have difficulty contacting you at school.
- Photographs should be black and white 5″ × 7″ (13 × 18 cms). Attach names and other relevant details of people in the photograph in order left to right, using a sticky label on the back. Do not write on the reverse as impression marks may damage the photograph. Also, it is a good idea to hold photographs by the edges to avoid getting finger-prints all over the front.
- In order to give you some control over when a story will appear, use an embargo. Write EMBARGO – *not for publication before . . .* (specify time or date). The paper will usually abide by this, although they are under no obligation to do so.
- Monitor the effectiveness of your press release distribution.

Table 5.1.2 *Checklist for writing a press release*

Find out which local papers have education correspondents or run regular features on schools. Try to use named contacts and build up a working relationship with them. Be professional and consistent in your dealings with them.

Don't forget: local press (include free papers); national press; professional journals (*Times Educational Supplement* and several others); Teachers' Unions publications. Your local reference library will have the addresses.

When dealing with the press on the telephone, never say 'No comment' in reply to a question. If the question cannot be immediately answered tell the reporter that you will ring back in, say, thirty minutes. This gives you time to consult, and to compose the reply *you* want. Be precise, clear, and positive.

Radio and TV

With the rapid increase of local radio (both BBC and independent) another market for your news has been established. Don't be afraid to use it – it is a powerful medium and can broadcast your news/ message to a very wide audience. Send the broadcasting companies a copy of your press releases. If you are asked to go to the studio to do a live or recorded interview, prepare yourself well beforehand.

- Know your subject.

- Find out how long you will be 'on air'.

- What questions will they ask you?

- Use notes if they will help you, but try not to shuffle the papers!

- Speak clearly, but relax if you can.

- Give yourself plenty of time to get to the studio if it is a live interview.

- Create pictures in words.

The radio station might want to send a reporter to the school to record the interview. Consider arrangements in advance.

- A quiet area for the interview to take place.

- Prime the participants fully.

- Pick your participants carefully, particularly the pupils.

- Find out time of broadcast and arrange for recording to be made.

It is less likely that TV will be involved in your marketing, but if you are thinking of approaching a TV station, or if the crew from the local newsdesk turns up, be sure that the 'story' is televisual – something with movement, colour, noise and activity, for example.

Television companies are often only interested in the 'scandal' or crisis story or that visit by Royalty/Secretary of State for Education. However, some schools do become subjects of documentary or current affairs programmes. My school was itself featured in a 'Panorama' profile in 1990. The disruption was extensive and the outcome questionable in PR value, apart from the promotional video that we produced from tapes which the BBC gave us. The 40-minute programme took two weeks to film and put our end-of-year planning back by a number of weeks. The message here is: think very hard before committing your staff and pupils to the cameras but if the chance does come, and the conditions are right, take it and keep a recording of it for future use.

The teacher as PR practitioner

Marketing schools is largely undertaken by committed amateurs, rather than by professionally trained PR and marketing specialists. You might be fortunate enough to secure the services of a professional, but it will be at a price.

Bearing these facts in mind, remember that first and foremost you are a teacher. You will not have an unlimited budget and a staff of dozens to do the donkey work. Therefore only so much is possible, and devoting an inordinate amount of time to marketing takes you away from your prime function in the school.

A word should be said about the legal implications of marketing for schools. The Institute of Public Relations (IPR) has a well-established Code of Practice adhered to by its professional practitioners. While much of this is specifically aimed at the business sector, one or two aspects of it are relevant to school managers in their role as marketers. Information on this can be obtained from the IPR at 15 Northburgh Street, London EC1V 0PR. Alternatively most books on business or industrial PR will have a summary of the Code.

- What exactly are you trying to achieve?
- For whom are you doing it?
- What and where is your market?
- What are you marketing? Is this what your 'customers' want?
- Have you a co-ordinated policy?
- Who will do the job?
- Have you the support of staff, senior management, governors?
- Will they be kept informed of progress or otherwise?
- Is a budget available for PR and marketing?
- Have you looked at your school from a visitor's point of view?
- What are your Unique Selling Points?
- Are you using all your business links effectively?
- Have you discussed the ethics of marketing a school? If not, why not?
- Are you prepared for disappointments?
- Are you prepared for a long-term commitment?
- What will be the effects on your job as a teacher?
- Have you, or will you get, administrative support?
- What are the high points of the school year?
- Who can be of help to you?
- How will you measure marketing effectiveness?
- Do you know the editors of your local papers?
- Where is your local radio station?
- Can you write a definition of marketing and PR?
- Could you say in a sentence or two what your school stands for?
- Do you know what your competitors are doing?
- How and where does marketing fit in with your school's development plan?
- What will happen if nothing happens?

Table 5.1.3 *Starter questions*

All the suggestions and strategies above have been tried and tested by many schools and have been found successful. For some it has been a matter of formalising and professionalising existing practice; for others it has opened up a whole new area of school management and experience. When you are successful in such a project, the rewards can be great, but be prepared for disappointments too. You will be embarking on long-term exercises and you won't win them all. With greater experience and knowledge, however, you should win more than you lose. Plan carefully, research your market, take risks, don't give up, evaluate thoroughly. The questions in Table 5.1.3 might help you start or find new directions to follow.

A final thought from the guru of business management, Peter Drucker:

> 'Marketing ... is not a specialised activity at all. It encompasses the whole business. It is the whole business seen from the point of view of its final result, that is of the customer's point of view. Concern and responsibility for marketing must therefore permeate all areas of the enterprise.'

Sponsorship for Schools

Laurence French

Marketing and public relations

Sponsorship, especially as part of a well-considered and carefully planned link between schools and businesses, can be an area of mutual benefit and opportunity. It should be seen as a part of the overall marketing and public relations (PR) plan rather than just simply as an activity to be entered into to gain much-needed extra funds for the school. To some extent many schools have sought sponsorship over the years – local businesses advertising in the school magazine or paying for the printing of the programme for the school play, for example. One of the main differences now is that sponsorship has been widened to encompass much more than the offsetting of minor expenditure; for some schools it is rapidly becoming their life-blood, especially for those whose pupil numbers are falling and, in consequence, so is their annual budget.

I shall explore below the wider aspects of sponsorship and give guidelines, based on personal experience of sponsorship, as to how schools and other organisations, whether they be businesses or non-commercial concerns, such as trusts or foundations, can work together for their mutual benefit. Sponsorship will form part of your PR campaign and needs to be understood as a management skill. The Institute of Public Relations (IPR) defines PR as: 'the deliberate, planned and sustained effort to establish and maintain mutual understanding between an organisation and its publics'.

Hard cash.

If you run your catering and facilities on cash payment, you know the problems. It can be embarrassing for subsidized students. Your staff have to collect it. Your accountants can miscount it. It's a constant security headache. And the shop around the corner competes with you for revenue. Not exactly the soft option, is it?

Now there's a solution. *Multicard* ™ is a cashless card payment system for machine vending or till payment. It can be coded for individual cardholders or for specific sites. It's easy to use, cost-efficient and discreet, eliminates the need for cash collection, and provides management information for error-free accounting.

It also controls student expenditure, keeping more of it within your premises.

Multicard ™ is already a success with schools, universities and large companies around Britain.

To find out how it can help you and your students call Carol Thornton at Mars Electronics International on 0734 697700, or Dick Boba at Powerhouse on 06285 31313.

MARS ELECTRONICS
international

The *Intelligent* Transaction

Easy money.

Sponsorship, and PR generally, need to be considered and planned for as carefully as any other activity that your school embarks on to involve those people who have an interest in your school – in other words your stakeholders. It will require hard work, commitment, an eye for the main chance, and perhaps no small amount of guile. If successful the rewards can be enormous.

What is sponsorship?

Sponsorship can comprise a number of elements. If it is considered to be simply the money paid by a company to boost the income of the school for some indeterminate purpose, this, while being a valid reason, misses several important points. Sponsorship is any or all of the items in Table 5.2.1. It will be clear from this list that these overlap somewhat, but it is important to be clear in your own mind what exactly you are asking from industry or commerce. The company will need to know exactly how you intend to use their personnel and for how long.

- Financial income: (a) gifts and donations; (b) covenants; (c) regular payments.
- Time: companies paying for their employees' time to come into school.
- Facilities: the availability of a company's facilities for school use and vice versa.
- Expertise: the use by a school of business/industrial experts.
- Equipment: the donation of equipment by a company for curricular use.
- Events: the support (financial or otherwise) of a school event by companies.
- Secondments: staff being seconded to business for training or work shadowing.

Table 5.2.1 *The elements of sponsorship*

Like most activities that schools embark on, the planning is all. In your marketing strategy you will have decided on a number of aims and objectives. The same applies to sponsorship. Know what you want to do before you start doing it. I would suggest three main objectives should be at the heart of your sponsorship planning:

1. to raise funds (or equipment, etc) for the school;

2. to raise the profile of the school in the local community and business sector;

3. to strengthen links between school and industry.

Sponsorship criteria

A Guide to Company Giving, edited by Michael Norton, sets out the criteria which need to be considered before applying for sponsorship (see Table 5.2.2).

Time scales will be important in your planning. Sponsorship by its very nature is usually a long-term project. Companies will have to be persuaded that your school is the one with which they wish to be associated. If your establishment does not have a particularly good image, then a marketing job and some high profile PR work will probably need to be undertaken before you can expect a positive response from businesses. The 'cap in hand approach' is rarely successful. It might elicit a one-off payment or piece of equipment, but what you should be aiming for is a long-term mutual

commitment which will result in partnership rather than patronage.

- Appropriateness of the activity/event to sponsor.
- Partnership, or are you simply asking for money?
- Real involvement by the sponsor.
- Continuity: is there scope for a long-term relationship?
- Initiative: something that would not happen without the company's support. Will they be supporting an initiative that they can look back on with pride and satisfaction?
- Visibility: what PR and specific publicity can be gained?
- Value for money: is the money to be used wisely and will the company get value for money?

Table 5.2.2 *Sponsorship criteria*

What have you to offer a sponsor?

Having established your aims and objectives you need to do an internal audit similar to the SWOT analysis that provided guidance for your marketing programme (see Table 5.2.3). Companies who

---

- What form of industrial/commercial links do you have? How long have they been in existence?
- Which are the major companies with whom you already have links?
- Have you had any successes that could be built on?
- Who can be of most use to you when considering companies with which to link or be associated? Consider your governors, staff, parents, pupils.
- Who will co-ordinate the project? Your marketing group might be appropriate.
- What are your unique selling points (USPs)? What have you got to offer that other schools have not?

Table 5.2.3 *Assessing your position*

- Are you an innovative school?
- Does your school have a particular philosophy or mission which is different or unique?
- What site facilities do you have which are special or attractive? eg disabled access.
- Have you a local or national reputation for, say, sports, art, music, technology, special needs?
- Are you regarded as a pioneering school in any way?

Table 5.2.4 *Assessing your USPs*

are themselves successful want to be associated with successful schools for all manner of reasons: to create goodwill; to be seen as good neighbours; because it is expected of them; because the Managing Director has a special interest in your school, and so on. In the present competitive climate it is likely that many schools will be marketing themselves vigorously in order to gain sponsorship links. If you head a school that has a particularly distinctive character or whose ethos is different from the rest, you might well stand a better chance of attracting a company to act as sponsor or partner. A survey of your unique selling points (USPs) will help you to see what you can offer (see Table 5.2.4).

If you consider your sponsorship link as a form of partnership you will need to think about what you can offer a company in return for their financial contributions. This may be a more difficult area to clarify, but it will need to be tackled. When approaching a company for sponsorship they will no doubt want to know what the *quid pro quo* will be. You might be surprised at what you can offer to industry if you put your mind to it. It will depend, of course, on the nature and level of sponsorship, but the points listed in Table 5.2.5 might aid your thinking.

It will depend on what you have available and how far you are prepared to go in order to strengthen the partnership with your sponsoring companies. The more you have to offer, the greater the negotiating strength you have. Don't forget that small and medium-sized companies do not have unlimited budgets and often welcome the offer of cheaper or free facilities or help with a project of some sort. Hiring facilities for courses, meetings or staff

- Carrying the company's name (on a minibus, a suite of rooms, programmes, etc).
- Putting school building/grounds at their disposal for social or training purposes (sports grounds, meeting rooms, conference facilities, short-course provision).
- Publicity for both organisations in the press, radio or television.
- Providing work experience pupils where appropriate.
- Providing future employees for the company.
- To be part of their industry – school programme (if they have one).
- Offering to undertake research projects for the company (a good GCSE or 'A' Level project for your students, perhaps?).
- Other help for which you have facilities (loaning of audio-visual material, printing facilities, loan of minibus for weekend/holiday use, catering).

Table 5.2.5 *What can you offer in return?*

conferences can be prohibitive. Your hall or teaching rooms might be just what they are looking for.

Approaching a sponsor

Having clearly thought out your plans, what you can offer in return, and the team who will be responsible for implementing the programme, the next step is deciding whom to approach and what to ask for. A register of local businesses (from the public reference library) will provide a comprehensive guide to the companies you can approach; your work experience/careers staff will also have a substantial list. Keep an eye on local business/industrial developments. Is there a new business park planned or being set up? Is there a redevelopment project in your area to attract new businesses? Even seemingly unrelated propositions, such as the planning of a new motorway or bypass, could have implications for local businesses. Are they moving in or out of the area as a consequence? Your local Chamber of Commerce and Planning Office will probably be able to offer some help here.

The companies you approach will expect you to be positive and

- Money for a specific piece of equipment.
- Funds to defray cost of trips, leaflets or other school publications.
- Help to stage events in school (plays, conferences, special visitors or guests).
- The purchase of specific books for specific courses.
- Help to buy a new school minibus.
- Sponsoring a student (or member of staff) on a course.
- Equipping classrooms or specific areas of the school with carpets, blinds, furniture, equipment.
- Help to fund a new course or pilot project.
- A contribution to prizes for Speech Day/Awards Day.
- Giving time and expertise in the classroom or on wider curriculum projects.
- Encouraging companies to advertise themselves at public functions for which the school would charge (careers conventions for example).
- Encouraging closer liaison with school by means of work experience placements.

Table 5.2.6 *Suitable items for sponsorship*

professional. Be certain what it is you are asking for and what use will be made of it. Table 5.2.6 suggests some of the projects and ideas you could consider.

Making contact

The initial approach to a company is very important and can vary according to the relationship you already have with them. Let us assume, for the sake of argument, that you are going to approach a company with which you have had no previous dealings. Do some market research first. Find out what they make or sell; whether they are an independent company or part of a larger corporation; if they have links with your competitors; what their attitude and policy is to education. Even the personal interests of the chairman can be of value if you can find these out. In one case a school which takes disabled pupils found a sympathetic ear from the chairman of a local firm who himself had a disabled daughter.

This information can often be found by means of a phone call to the company before mentioning the word 'sponsorship'. The more you find out about a company, the easier will be the approach when you broach the subject of money or equipment. During the course of the phone call, find out to whom you should write – name and position. It is best to go to the top if possible – the MD or chairman.

The letter which follows should be brief but concise (see Table 5.2.7). A follow-up phone call might be necessary to gain personal contact if the reply to your letter is not immediately forthcoming. Try to arrange a face-to-face meeting with your contact as soon as possible.

Once contact has been made it will be necessary to maintain and foster it. Invite the person involved to your school; if a school function is imminent, that can provide a good excuse for a visit. Don't forget the thanking letter if the company shows interest.

Timing is important if you are asking for money. Budgets are often decided as early as November or December for the following April financial year. It would be advisable to prepare the application in June or July ready for the autumn term.

Where your project goes from there will depend on the reaction of the company, your own persistence and the relationship you form with the representative of the firm. However, it might be

---

- Introduce yourself and your school.
- State your business clearly and succinctly. Be specific about how much you want, not forgetting to say how the money would be spent and why you think the company might be interested in supporting your school.
- Use headed paper and do not write more than one side of A4 if possible.
- Use a typwriter or word processor.
- Address the letter 'For the personal attention of . . .'
- Send them information about your school – brochures, recent press cuttings.
- Engender a feeling of urgency about the appeal.

Table 5.2.7 *The approach letter*

quite a long time before you are in the position to ask for money. The firm needs to be sure of you; you, in turn, need to be certain of your position. Just as the manager will consult with his/her colleagues, you should do the same, remembering the vital importance and approval of the governors. Keep staff informed and try to create an attitude of 'ownership' among the staff. Involve people at all levels and delegate responsibilities for the handling of the contact once it has been established.

Many companies have community or educational budgets and are desperate to be linked with schools in some way. Sainsbury's, for example, are big supporters of the arts and music, and many schools have benefited from their generosity. Many large national or international companies have such a scheme and support educational/cultural causes. With the climate moving towards one of social responsibility by many more companies, a link with a school can be one way in which industry or commerce can discharge its responsibility, and in many cases they need us as much as we need them. The most valuable 'commodity' that we in education possess is the future workforce upon which they will draw.

It may be that the company approaches you initially, having heard of you through the press or by word of mouth. This approach can actually work in your favour as the company will probably have not thought out its approach quite so clearly as you would have done if the roles were reversed, and you can, therefore, take the lead and negotiate quite a favourable deal for yourself.

Ethical considerations

Raising revenue through sponsorship can be a tricky business and subject to all sorts of unforseen difficulties, particularly the ethical points that may be put in your way. One of the most difficult tasks at first will be selling the idea to the staff, some of whom, I can tell you from personal experience, will be absolutely opposed to any financial arrangements with business. It is important that these views are considered and discussed; therefore you need to be very sure of your own commitment to the scheme. Choice of companies will be important. The ethics of sponsorship need to be discussed with your staff, and a school must not link with firms that can in any way compromise its integrity – cigarette manufacturers or breweries, for example. A more ambivalent relationship might be sponsorship with a condom manufacturer. Schools in New York, for example, promote condoms as part of their anti-Aids drive.

It is important also that whatever revenue is generated, it is used for the good of the pupils or to enhance the curriculum. A new Swedish-designed desk for the head's office is hardly appropriate ethical use of funds!

Legal considerations

There are several legal points that need to be considered too (see Table 5.2.8).

---

1. There must be a declaration by any member of your school (staff, governing body or other interested parties) of financial interest in the sponsoring company. A failure to do this led to unfortunate publicity when a school unthinkingly attempted to woo parents with vouchers for a local company, a senior manager of whom was on the governing body.

2. Any financial benefit derived from sponsorship must be itemised in the school's accounts for the auditors.

3. You need to be aware of copyright legislation in any literature that is being reproduced about your school or the sponsoring company.

4. If you enter into a sponsorship deal, a legal contract protects both parties. A commercial solicitor will advise you on this.

5. Be sure that you take steps to ensure that your reputation does not suffer if things go wrong.

6. Insurance for events if the school is the sponsor – are non-teachers covered under school insurance policy or by their own company's policy?

7. Insurance for equipment lent by companies – who is covered for what? And for how much?

8. If a member of staff is seconded to industry as part of a sponsorship deal, check that they are covered under the company's employee insurance scheme.

Table 5.2.8 *Legal considerations*

Professional business managers

Some schools have gone to the lengths of employing business managers to run their revenue-raising activities. They are usually paid on a commission basis, but some are salaried members of staff. Either way, I am sceptical about some of the claims and the principle of employing such people. If they are any good, they will cost you at least £20,000 a year and will have to raise a great deal more than that to justify their existence.

As I have stated already, I believe sponsorship is about partnership between schools and industry which spans a wide variety of activities, not just the exercise of entrepreneurial skills in raising funds. As teachers we are in the best position to know how the school will benefit from its industrial links and what it can do for its sponsoring companies. Trust your own judgement as a professional educator and manager. In return I believe companies are more likely to respond positively to you as a teacher than they would to a business manager whom they will probably see as a person with little or no interest in or knowledge of education.

Patience and perseverance

Finally, businesses have been going through a deep recession in recent years and many will just not have the money available for sponsorship. They have faced financial cut backs, and are naturally keen to safeguard their own workforce first, before committing funds to sponsoring projects. The bigger the company, the more likely will be your success, but nevertheless do not disregard your local small/medium-size businesses. Be persistent; you will be embarking on a long-term project and success can take many different forms.

Further reading

Norton, Michael (ed), *A Guide to Company Giving*, Directory of Social Change (1990);
Fitzherbert, Luke & Eastwood, Michael (eds), *A Guide to Major Trusts* Directory of Social Change (1990). Both available from local libraries or from: The Directory of Social Change, Radius Works, Back Lane, London NW3 1HL. £14.95 each.

Part Six

Managing Property, Premises and Resources

BUSHBOARD

Bushboard is the leading UK manufacturer of high quality laminate faced products and components. Bushboard has now become market leader in cubicle and washroom systems, developing further systems for this and other markets, some of which are shown on this page.

This page shows the Bushboard range of cubicles and washrooms, designed to cover virtually all requirements, together with other interior products. **If you have any queries relating to these systems, or require brochures, please contact our Marketing Department on**

0933 224983

Product features include:

- Hardware for easy use by the disabled
- Half-height ducts
- Easy clean surfaces and ducting

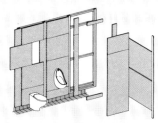

BB1 PLUS

A Fast Track cubicle and washroom system, specifically developed to combine design flair, economy and ex-stock availability. A choice of over 100 colourways is available direct from Bushboard.

PROFILES

Purpose made for use in leisure facilities where attractive appearance cannot be sacrificed in favour of physical durability. Profiles leisure cubicles feature a wide range of colourways and fascia shapes, the whole system manufactured in solid grade laminate.

BB4 SPEED

A completely integrated laminate based cubicle and washroom system, giving versatile design, combined with practical solutions. Speedy identification of a huge range of laminate components results in short lead times for what is essentially a bespoke system.

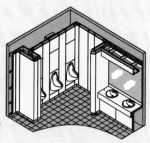

INTERIOR FINISHES

Bushboard's specialist division in the design, manufacture and installation of laminate finishes to suit "on-site" requirements.

Bushboard Parker Ltd.
Rixon Road,
Finedon Road Industrial Estate,
Wellingborough,
Northants NN8 4BA

BushBoard®

A Kingsway Group Company

Telephone: (0933) 224983 Telex: 31684 BUSHWB G Fax: (0933) 223553

142

6.1

Management of Buildings

Jim Donnelly

Managing the school buildings has always been a concern of the head, though in recent years this has often been delegated to a deputy. However, the exercise of this management responsibility has been circumscribed by the fact that not only did the LEA hold the purse strings, but also in many cases they paid little attention to the views of the school in deciding where priorities for spending lay. The LEA took a global view of their 'stock' of schools, whereas the head and deputies were responsible only for their own particular workplace. Managing buildings thus became a game – in which some heads and deputies developed considerable skill in finding out what money was available, who had control of it and what *their* priorities were. By skilful manipulation you might get several classrooms refitted (the Area Officer), a new alarm system installed (County Hall Health and Safety Officer) and a new lathe (the Craft, Design and Technology Adviser). You also learned that sometimes there was money available at the end of the financial year if you could find out who had it!

Schemes of delegation

Local Management of Schools (LMS) has changed this – but only up to a point. This is because most schemes of delegation divide the responsibility for maintenance of buildings between the school (the 'inside') and the LEA (the 'outside'); it is only for those parts which

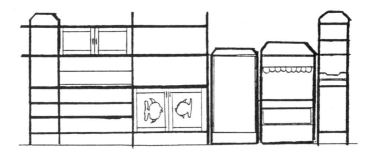

NATIONAL GALLERY

Graffiti Clean have several services available not only for building cosmetics, but for Health & Safety of occupants too.

With new services to combat SICK BUILDING SYNDROME

GRAFFITI REMOVAL
ANTI - GRAFFITI PROTECTION
STONE AND BRICK CLEANING
ASBESTOS ROOF CLEANING AND COATING
(SBS)   WATER TANK CLEANING AND REFURBISHMENT
(SBS)   FIRE AND FLOOD DAMAGE
(SBS)   AIR CONDITIONING VIDEO SURVEY AND CLEANING

Affordable maintenance programmes available to keep buildings clean and healthy.

GRAFFITI CLEAN LIMITED
UNIT 5, 124A WOODHILL,
HILLREACH, LONDON.
SE18 5JL

TEL: 081 855 0008
FAX: 081 855 0330

fall within the direct control of the school that there will be money in the school budget. (While this section deals with county schools, it is important to recognise that there are different divisions of responsibility with voluntary-aided, special agreement and grant-maintained schools.)

The first step in managing the buildings should therefore be to examine the exact nature of the agreement under which the school operates. This will make clear what the school will have to pay for. Examples of the way responsibilities are divided can be seen in the box which gives an extract from DES Circular No 7/88, dealing with electrical services.

LEA	SCHOOL
Emergency and time systems (except for any systems purchased at school cost)	Alarms and fire detection systems; minor repairs to clocks and bells; maintenance of any systems purchased at school cost

It can be readily seen that a dialogue between school and LEA will be necessary at points of overlap. The definition of 'minor repairs', for example, will be critical to the school. If the school wants something done in a hurry it may be necessary to be flexible in one's interpretation.

The interface between LEA and school has already given rise to some interesting issues. For example, in one school the library roof leaked and damaged the floor. The floor was wood-block, covered by carpet. Who should have paid for the repairs? The floor was the LEA's responsibility but was wood-block a floor covering (and hence the school's responsibility) or was it structural (and hence the LEA's)? The matter was further complicated by the fact that the real damage to the carpet was caused not by the rain falling on top of it but by the wood-block expanding underneath it! The LEA was holding central insurance cover for its part but the school had a separate policy for the contents; thus the issue mattered to the insurers and ultimately to the school. The LEA ruled that the woodblock was a floor covering and that the school was therefore responsible for it: the latter would have to pay for the replacement of the carpet. It was decided not to replace the woodblock and so the sequence of events will not be repeated, in that school's library at any rate. Fortunately the school's insurers accepted the LEA's interpretation and eventually refunded the money for the carpet, although the school initially had to pay for it without any guarantee that this would happen. The point of this anecdote is to emphasise the necessity of establishing as clearly as possible where the demarcation lines are drawn: be clear what the school budget is for.

The next stage is to find out what the LEA plans to spend on the outside of the buildings. Ask to meet the Maintenance Officer and try to get some answers about where his/her priorities lie for your school for the next year and beyond. Try to ensure that such priorities tie in with the school's, if necessary by bargaining. It is essential that governors (including LEA nominees) are involved in this process. If it seems necessary, confirm any promises in writing.

The school maintenance budget

Having ascertained where the school's responsibilities lie it is necessary for the governors to plan a maintenance programme. The first thing is *not* to decide how to spend the money but instead to turn to the school's vision statement, whether it is expressed in these terms or not. (LMS is about management, *not* about money). It is important to be as far-sighted as one can about curricular needs in the future since this will dictate how rooms and other areas are to be used. The vision is also likely to include a mention of the environment in which staff and students are to work. These are important parameters in identifying priorities for expenditure under any budget heading, and none more so than here.

Many governing bodies delegate the responsibility for the maintenance budget to a sub-committee. The sub-committee can then set out its priorities, preferably for more than one year. Every school will have its own order of priority but Table 6.1.1 gives an example of how it can be set out.

This simple priority list is then used when requests for expenditure are made. The senior staff have a clear rationale for any decisions, with the authority to act right away when vandalism occurs. Some schools are already finding that it is sensible to look at the items under 3, 4 and 5 later in the financial year when the needs under 1 and 2 are clearer.

Staff need to be aware of the policy. They will find it easier to cope

---

MAINTENANCE PRIORITIES OF 'THIS SCHOOL', 1992/93

1. Removal of all graffiti, both internal and external, as soon as it appears.

2. Immediate repair of broken windows and damaged doors.

3. Maintenance of appearance of all 'public' areas (for example, the entrance hall).

4. Refurbishment within each department/faculty, in consultation with the staff concerned, on a planned basis.

5. Improvements to 'public' areas.

Table 6.1.1 *Maintenance priorities*

with less than ideal surroundings if they know that at least there are plans to ameliorate them to some degree in the future. If they are involved in setting priorities – as suggested in the example above – this will have a beneficial effect on morale.

Students should also be aware of their importance in maintaining pleasant working conditions. Schools with positive policies find that, for example, graffiti in the school is much reduced, at least inside the building.

There needs to be a clear understanding within the school of where responsibility for decision-making lies. Obviously the total budget for maintenance will have been set by the governors, and guidelines such as those suggested above may exist. However, it also needs to be clear who can authorise this expenditure. Is it the head, or a nominated deputy, or the caretaker? Whom do staff inform about broken windows or graffiti? How do staff have an input into the planning of the expenditure on improvements?

How to avoid trouble

For items of expenditure in excess of certain sums, the LEA financial regulations are likely to indicate particular procedures. For example, there may be a requirement that two or more quotations are obtained for work in excess of a certain amount (a wise move in any case) and there may be a list of approved contractors.

In some schools, a noticeable result of LMS has been the

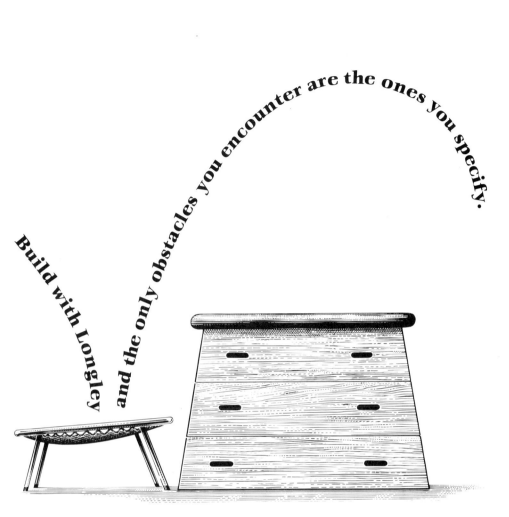

Build with Longley and the only obstacles you encounter are the ones you specify.

From sports halls and swimming pools to new classroom blocks – from modernisation to refurbishment – you can't beat the Longley team.

Our track record in school building is second to none. We've been a major player for over 125 years and understand the disciplines and strengths required for school projects.

We have a full range of talents to exercise on your next project, however testing. With our experience, every move is executed cost-effectively. And with our emphasis on timing – you're sure to get a winning result: the building you want on time and on budget, with no obstacles.

149

appointment of a part-time handyman or a caretaker/handyman, who can undertake minor improvements. If this is contemplated, one needs to be very clear about the implications for financial control (one cannot just hand a caretaker £20 out of one's back pocket!) and legal responsibility (both towards the employee and to anyone who is hurt as a result of negligent workmanship). One needs to examine these issues very carefully *before* any problems arise; it is likely to be too late afterwards.

CHECKLIST

1. Have regard to the school's vision/aims.

2. Involve governors and staff.

3. Plan in advance.

4. Produce written policy on priorities.

5. Make staff roles clear.

6. Involve students in the care of the school.

Opportunities for Energy Efficiency in Schools

Mukund Patel

Much of our present lifestyle depends on the availability of abundant energy supplies. Unfortunately, the era of cheap and plentiful energy has come to an end; we now urgently need to conserve energy.

The White Paper on the environment clearly states that the government is keen to encourage energy efficiency. Schools have a significant role to play here: they are in a unique position, not only to save energy but also to develop energy awareness in education of children.

The scope for savings

With energy costs forming a small but nonetheless significant part of all school budgets, there are three main reasons for schools to consider ways of reducing this expenditure:

- measures taken to reduce energy consumption may lead to expenditure savings that can be used for other resources in schools;

- to a large extent, energy is derived from non-renewable fossil-fuel sources and schools have a contribution to make in reducing demand for fossil fuels;

- global warming is a matter of increasing concern – energy conservation measures taken by schools can reduce the direct and indirect emission of CO_2, a major greenhouse gas.

Until recently, fuel was considered to be a relatively cheap commodity and little attention was paid to the need to design or manage schools to limit consumption. As a result there is considerable scope for savings in this area in existing school buildings.

Nationally, LEAs devote approximately 3 per cent of annual expenditure to energy. In 1988/89 this accounted for expenditure of £315 million, about three times the expenditure on text and library books in that year.

The above figure indicates an average expenditure on energy in a 240-pupil primary school of about £10,000 per year, and in a 1000-pupil secondary of about £38,000 per year. Small percentage savings on expenditure of this order would release significant sums which – in the context of LMS – could be devoted to other needs in the school.

Significant factors

These average figures conceal wide variations about the norm, variations which are a reflection of three factors:

- the amount of accommodation provided in relation to the number of pupils;

- the form and construction of the buildings;

- the management of buildings.

All these factors can be influenced to some extent by the individual school under LMS.

Accommodation-to-pupil ratio

There is now a real incentive for schools to identify steps that can be taken to reduce the amount of accommodation used. For example, on average, a typical classroom accounts for energy expenditure in the order of £300 per annum. Thus the removal of one temporary classroom might result in immediate annual savings of this order (or more, depending upon fuel used and thermal characteristics of the temporary classroom).

Are your fuel bills going through the roof?

Even well-insulated school and college buildings will use a lot more energy than necessary when there are no effective heating controls installed. With modern controls fitted you can start spending less money on energy and more on educational equipment.

Landis & Gyr is Europe's leader in the manufacture, installation and service of heating controls for all types of building. We offer a detailed service to individual schools which enables significant energy savings to be made – whether it's the fitting of simple timeswitches or sophisticated computer based energy management systems.

The level of automation that can now be achieved even gives scope for increased productivity amongst staff who look after the buildings.

Landis & Gyr offer:

- **National coverage through 6 regional offices.**
- **Advice on all heating control systems.**
- **Replacement controls and spares.**
- **Controls commissioning.**
- **Flexible maintenance packages.**

For all heating control information and assistance, contact your nearest Regional Office at:

Cumbernauld (0236) 737344   *Newcastle-upon-Tyne* 091-268 8586
Leeds (0532) 350704   *Handforth* 061-488 4044
Willenhall (0902) 305577   *Bristol* (0272) 724472
                      or *Bourne End* (0628) 850840

Landis & Gyr Building Control (UK) Ltd
Dukes Meadow, Millboard Road
Bourne End, Bucks SL8 5XF

LANDIS & GYR

Leading Europe in Building Control

Alterations

Alterations to the fabric of the building can also result in direct savings in energy consumption; the capital expenditure can often be justified in relation to these savings. Short-term paybacks can be achieved by modest measures such as draught stripping of windows and better controls on heating plant. Longer-term paybacks can be expected through such measures as roof insulation, upgrading heating installations and major alterations to the buildings. Schools are in a good position to identify such measures and to encourage those responsible to take appropriate action.

When alterations and additions to existing buildings are carried out schools may be able to influence the design of such works to ensure that energy consumption is fully considered. The Architects and Building Branch of the DES has recently published its 'Guide to Energy Efficient Refurbishment', which gives extensive guidance on measures to reduce energy consumption.

Building management

Improved management of the building can lead to immediate economies in energy consumption without the need for capital expenditure. The Audit Commission has estimated that there is scope for a 10 per cent reduction in energy consumption through better housekeeping measures. These include:

- closing windows and doors in cold weather;
- checking thermostat and time-control setting;
- switching off lights when not needed;
- attending to leaks promptly;
- discouraging use of unauthorised heaters;
- checking hot water temperature and reducing it if necessary.

A 10 per cent saving in energy consumption related to the examples cited above represents approximately £1,000 per annum for the 240-pupil primary school and nearly £4,000 per annum for the 1000-pupil secondary school.

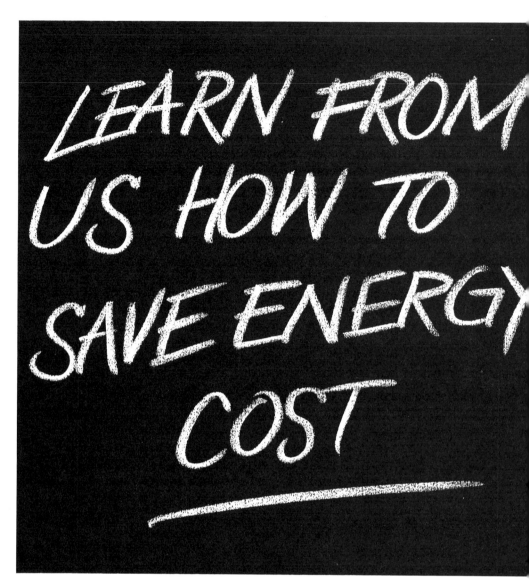

LEARN FROM US HOW TO SAVE ENERGY COST

If you could cut energy costs, think what you could spend the savings

The Electricity companies can help you to improve energy efficien through management, building and heating system design and the cho of energy efficient replacement equipment such as point-of-use hot wat

DRYMEN PRIMARY SCHOOL

We've helped dozens of schools become energy efficient - and these two have won national awards. Fax for our information pack on 071-233 7330. It could be a real education.

MILL HILL COUNTY PRIMARY SCH

PLANELECTR

Achievements to date

Schools have already achieved substantial reductions in energy consumption. In 1985/6 they spent £43 million less on energy than they did in 1978/9.

The savings achieved so far have been significant and confirm the potential for further progress. They represent a substantial contribution to the national effort to reduce the consumption of fossil fuels and the emission of greenhouse gases. The savings achieved since 1978/9 represent the equivalent of 290,000 tonnes of coal, and a reduction in CO_2 emissions of between 348,000 and 500,000 tonnes.

Summary

Energy expenditure represents a significant element in school budgets.

Savings in energy expenditure can allow funds to be transferred to other areas of expenditure.

There is scope for substantial savings in energy expenditure in schools.

Schools can achieve savings in energy expenditure through:

- reducing the amount of accommodation occupied;

- identifying short-term payback opportunities;

- identifying longer-term payback opportunities;

- ensuring energy consumption is considered in the design of extensions and alterations;

- introducing improved energy management;

- improving comfort conditions by ensuring that schools are not overheated;

- raising the awareness of staff and pupils to the importance of energy conservation.

Schools can contribute to the national and global need to conserve fossil fuels and to reduce the emission of greenhouse gases.

Note: The Architects and Building Branch of the DES has produced a number of publications on the subject of energy efficiency and is also participating in a 1992 series of regional seminars on energy efficiency. Further information is available from: Architects and Building Branch, Department of Education and Science, Rooms 7/21, Elizabeth House, York Road, London SE1 7PH.

6.3

Energy Management in Schools

Jennifer Hands

At the same time as employing the basic energy-saving measures outlined in the previous chapter, it is wise to ascertain if the heating system offers a means of control through time switching, or thermostats or thermostatic radiator valves.

Time switches

Time switches are a very cost-effective means of saving energy. They are not expensive to buy and install and ensure that the plant is not brought into action too early.

Normally the switch-on time is designed to start the plant in time for the space temperature to be comfortable when school starts. In the winter the pre-heat period is geared to the coldest day. However, on mild days the same switch-on time will warm the school up more quickly and it will be comfortable several hours before occupation. This wastes energy.

The answer is to use an optimiser: a self-learning adjustable time switch. This takes into account the inside (and often the outside) temperature and adjusts the switch-on time accordingly so that the school gets suitably comfortable at the same time each day. The optimiser saves energy because it starts the plant at the most appropriate time each day – much later on mild days than on cold days – thus reducing the pre-heating time.

Time switches and optimisers can both be set to take into account the different needs of weekdays and weekends and to provide an

extended pre-heat period on Monday mornings.

If you have no time switches at all, savings of at least 50 per cent on your energy bills would be quite possible – assuming that the plant is currently allowed to run all the time. If you change from time switching to optimised controls a saving of 10–20 per cent should be possible.

Weather compensators

A further method of saving energy would be to use an outside or weather compensator. This would lower the temperature of water supplied to radiators as the outside temperature rose so that it is hotter in cold weather and not so hot in mild conditions. Again, the correct amount of heat is provided at the right time, energy is saved and the internal environment is improved. In particular, a compensator can reduce heat wastage from exposed pipework between radiators.

Zoning

As there are likely to be some spaces which are not being used all the time, consider inserting additional valves, switches or thermostats into pipework in certain areas so that these can be controlled individually. For example, rooms to be used for evening classes may be heated without having to heat other areas as well. Zoning can also avoid over-heating through solar gains if one side of the building receives more sunshine than another.

Conclusion

All the above improvements will save money; the payback period on investment made is normally between one and two years, although this depends on the condition of each installation. It's important to obtain the best professional advice to ensure money is well spent.

The division of responsibilities between schools and LEAs under LMS schemes means, of course, that schools pay running costs while LEAs are responsible for installing energy-saving devices and generally improving heating systems. This is an area where it is

very clear that governors need to discuss these matters with their LEA and try to insist on improvements being made where possible. In many LEAs, a positive relationship is likely to lead to joint actions, with the school possibly making some contribution from their delegated budget where they can see obvious reductions in their energy costs. Where this relationship does not exist it may be necessary to shout loudly about the waste of money and energy, given that we live in times when such 'green' issues are so important.

6.4

Energy Savings in Lighting*

Lighting accounts for 15 per cent of total UK electricity consumption. In offices and classrooms it often amounts to 50 per cent of energy costs. Yet energy-saving in this area is extremely straightforward and will usually pay for itself within two years.

Generally, the older the existing system, the greater the saving that can be made. Some overhauls can reduce costs by 75 per cent, but even fluorescent lighting as little as two years old can now be replaced by modern systems 30 per cent more efficient.

The chart below shows what to look for in terms of costly, obsolete lighting – and how to gain most from its replacement.

Renewing the lighting system can bring other advantages. As well as being ecologically preferable, there are likely benefits in terms of:

- improved productivity – having the right kind of lighting for each activity clearly makes sense in terms of enhancing the work environment;

- reduced maintenance – modern, energy-efficient lighting will require fewer repairs and less frequent replacement;

- lower incidence of crime, vandalism and accidents – better lighting deters the vandal and increases confidence in personal safety;

- a more pleasant work environment.

---

* This article has been adapted from a booklet produced by the Lighting Industry Federation entitled *Energy Managers' Lighting Handbook.*

APPLICATION		WHAT TO LOOK FOR
General		Any lighting more than 10 years old
		Fluorescent tubes with bayonet cap connections
		Badly discoloured plastic diffusers or painted shades and reflectors
		Lighting as recent as 5 years old
		1½ inch (38mm) diameter fluorescent tubes
		Ordinary filament light bulbs
Industrial		Mercury fluorescent lamp bulbs (MBF type): 'blue' mercury lights
		Mercury/tungsten 'blended' lamps (MBTL type)
		Old 8 foot 125W fluorescent fittings
		High wattage light bulbs (300W to 1500W filament lamps)
Commercial		2 foot 40W fluorescent lamps
		Old 8 foot 125W fluorescent fittings
		Fluorescent fittings with opal diffusers
		'De Luxe' warm-tone fluorescent lamps
Display		PAR 38 sealed beam reflector lamps
		Reflector lamps
Outdoor Including amenity and security		Filament lamps (light bulbs)
Floodlighting		High wattage filament lamps
		Tungsten halogen floodlights
Control of lighting		Large areas controlled by 'a switch near the door'
		Lighting that has no 'middle way' between all-on or all-off
		Lights blazing away outside normal working hours
		Installations that benefit from significant daylight provision

Energy Savings in Lighting

WHAT YOU SHOULD DO		HOW YOU BENEFIT
Without question: have it replaced immediately Get an expert survey done to assess the opportunities for energy-saving lighting refurbishment		• Refurbishment installations commonly produce 60% energy savings and paybacks in less than 18 months • Dramatic improvement of lighting quality is likely • High probability of major cost savings plus much better lighting
Replace them with compact fluorescent lamps in the same fittings, or if necessary renew the fittings Replace with PAR-E or with low-voltage tungsten halogen lighting or metal halide discharge lighting		• Immediate energy cost savings of 75%, plus reduced maintenance through much longer lamp life • Overall lighting cost can be cut by half, at low capital cost
For most 'high bay' applications, replace them with high pressure sodium (SON) lighting For low mounting heights, replace with either high pressure sodium (SON) lighting or modern fluorescent lighting		• SON gives satisfactory colour rendering in most industrial applications, and is very energy effective • High frequency electronic or low-loss fluorescent lighting gives energy costs almost as low as SON lighting, plus excellent colour rendering
Replace with modern louvred or high-performance prismatic lens fittings using power-saving 'triphosphor' lamps High frequency electronic or low-loss ballasts can be particularly effective Metal halide and SON uplighters for certain applications		• Energy savings of 30-45% are commonly achieved, with much improved lighting quality - benefits include elimination of glare, flicker and hum; easy starting and good colour rendering
Replace with PAR-E or with low-voltage tungsten halogen lighting or metal halide discharge lighting		• Energy saving of 30-75% for equivalent lighting performance
Install new lighting using SON high pressure sodium or SOX low pressure sodium lamps, or compact fluorescent lamps		• Energy savings of 75-85%, and lower maintenance through longer lamp life, plus better lighting
Replace with SON high pressure sodium or mercury discharge lighting		• Energy savings of 60-80%, plus better lighting
Get an expert to survey how you use and control the lighting in your premises		• Eliminating energy waste by use of modern control systems can reduce electricity consumption by typically 25-60% • And provide better working conditions

The Kogan Page Careers Series

Enrol the largest UK lamp manufacturer as your supplier for better lighting with greater economy

GE Thorn

Thorn Lamps Miles Road Mitcham Surrey CR4 3YX Tel 081-640 1221 Fax 081-685 9625

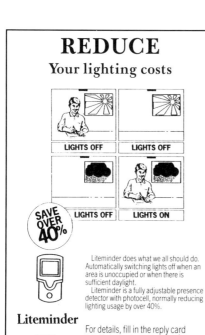

Water Management

Derek Plimley

Money down the drain

With all larger educational institutions operating their water supply through a metered system, water management can offer a rapid return on investment. Wastage exists principally in urinal cisterns flushing away every 15 minutes throughout the day. This amounts to 45 litres per hour going down the drain, 24 hours per day. At a conservative estimate of 50 pence per 1000 litres, (costs vary considerably from area to area) over the course of a year each cistern is consuming over £250 of the school budget. With the cost of water set to increase at 5 per cent above the level of inflation per annum, the need to make savings is clear.

With cisterns operating 80 per cent of the time unnecessarily, the payback period for the installation of a water-management system can often be expected to be less than 12 months. The method of operation of such systems will vary from one manufacturer to another. Some operate on time switch technology with additional 'service' flushes to ensure drainage levels are maintained. Most, however, operate using infra-red detectors where operation when vacant is limited to service flushes only. Often such systems are battery-operated which further reduces installation cost while ensuring a safe low-voltage installation. With an extensive battery-life, servicing is not a problem.

A saving of £250 and above can be expected for every cistern in operation. A payback period of less than 12 months is not unusual, dependent upon the efficiency of the system chosen and the cost of water per cubic metre. But for any school operating six or more cisterns, £1,500 per year could be 'going down the drain' when it could be used for more educational purposes.

Investment and payback periods

On the subject of energy management it is true to say that, regardless of whether it is the school head or the local authority engineer who initiates energy savings, it is vital for the school to realise capital investment and payback periods. From a position of such knowledge, the school will know when they can realistically expect to see additional funds made available for more direct educational expenditure. Without such knowledge, these sums may not be reallocated back to the school but placed elsewhere by the local authorities.

While local authorities are hard pressed in many areas, the correct legislation allows individual schools to initiate savings now and see the financial benefit sooner. LMS allows schools responsibility for capital expenditure when a net saving is the end result. In the event of a payback period of over 12 months, monies may be borrowed from the local authority to avoid accessing the maintenance budget. Clearly this is an important area where, across the board, thousands of pounds could be ploughed back in to the educational establishment.

Risk Management for Schools

Alastair Buchan

Schools now pay for all day-to-day crime. On average they can expect to spend a third of their maintenance budget on crime-related expenditure. The implications are clear.

Risk management is simply the assessment of the global risk to a school, its occupants and facilities, and the taking of all reasonably practicable steps to minimise possible losses.

Aims, methods and strategy

It helps to have a clear, unambiguous aim. Something like 'To ensure that the risk of loss or injury to the building, its facilities, equipment and occupants does not exceed acceptable levels' should have the support of your governors and staff.

Part of a risk-management policy statement should outline the methods you intend to use to reach your goal. Topics which should be covered are:

- procedures to be followed by staff, pupils and visitors;

- staff training;

- education;

- the role of the community.

There must also be an overall strategy where the various elements

171

PORTASTOR®

HIGH SECURITY CABINETS

THE HEAD TEACHER'S WORKSTATION

Proven

- **IDEAL** FOR LOCAL FINANCIAL MANAGEMENT SYSTEMS AND CONFIDENTIAL INFORMATION.

- **PERFECT** FOR PROTECTING ALL SCHOOL COMPUTERS, VIDEO RECORDERS & TAPES, AND AV & CDT EQUIPMENT.

- **LARGER** INSTOR   WALK-IN SECURE STORES ALSO AVAILABLE

For more details contact **Richard Lewis** on **0904 624872**
or write to PORTASTOR HIGH SECURITY PRODUCTS (4/E033/6)
PORTASILO LTD, FREEPOST, YORK YO1 1US.

PORTA-, PORTASTOR & INSTOR are registered trademarks   © Portasilo Limited 1990

fit together regardless of who is responsible for paying the bill. Shared responsibility is not just between individual schools and LEAs. Countermeasures at your school can divert them to the school down the road. This displacement of crime brings no significant, sustained downturn in the figures, especially when the school down the road displaces its crime to you. Effective security comes from cooperation between all concerned.

Cooperation by itself is not enough, however. Risk management is a long-term commitment. The school criminal is persistent. Just because a countermeasure is successful today does not mean it will be tomorrow. Good security demands constant vigilance. There must be a steady interchange of ideas, information and resources between all agencies concerned.

Identification and reduction of risk

Before deciding on an acceptable level of risk, identify the risks you wish to take into account. These may vary from school to school, the most common being:

- trespass;
- criminal damage (usually called 'vandalism');
- theft;
- burglary;
- fire (including arson);
- assault;
- personal injury.

Risks can be linked: trespass can lead to criminal damage that turns into theft which encourages burglary that prompts arson and leads to the caretaker being bashed over the head as the criminals make their escape.

In theory, action to stop the trespasser will break this chain at source; in practice, what will stop the trespasser will not deter the burglar.

Action taken to reduce a risk should be commensurate with the expected level of loss from that risk. (Put another way, it should be in keeping with the criminal's expected gains.) It must also be part

176

of an overall strategy where the steps taken to minimize one risk reinforce action taken to reduce others.

Levels of risk

Once you have prepared your list of risks you must assess the level of each. This must be based on fact, not opinion, impressions, or anecdotes – or fear of what might happen if the sky falls in.

You must know *what* has happened, *when* it happened and *what it cost*, either in cash or lost facilities. This means examining what has happened at your school over the last year or so. When you have established the pattern of crime, you can begin looking for trends and asking if this model will change, and how. Proper recording will give you a record of the type of incident which leads to loss and the scale and frequency of that loss. Crime report forms are valuable since they ensure that the information is recorded in a standard format and like can be compared to like.

Some changes in risk can be anticipated. If you plan to turn a classroom into a computer suite and order 20 computers, the risk of theft from that room is going to increase. Some action should perhaps be taken *before* the computers arrive – even if it means buying 18 computers and using the money earmarked for the other two to provide protection.

When you have assessed the risks it is possible to make some estimate of the priority each should be given by rating the frequency, the cost of countermeasures and the possible loss of each as high, medium or low.

Unless resources are abundant beyond dreams, it is unwise to spend money trying to prevent trespass before burglary.

Your options

You have now identified and measured the risks. What are you going to do with this information? You have four options.

- Do nothing:
  - the level of risk does not justify action;
  - there is no cost-effective action.

- Avoid the risk:
  - if you do not have computers, they cannot be stolen.

Card Systems Division Unit 7, Canada Road
Byfleet, Weybridge,
Surrey KT14 7JL

NBS – The Multi-function ID Card Solution

The multi-function Identification Card is becoming a feature of everyday life. Employers and employees alike are increasingly turning to electronic card activated systems for security and a multitude of other facilities.

Converted Photographic ID Systems lack the ability to provide high security and do not lend themselves to the production of multi-function cards. In addition they are expensive to run, messy and present storage, filing and retrieval problems.

Today's security and identification applications demand flexibility, efficiency, accuracy and superior price performance.

NBS were quick to recognise these facts and develop the technology to provide total integrated solutions – NBS Mosaic Digital Imaging systems.

Utilising sophisticated proprietary and standard imaging technologies together with NBS's application software and expertise. Mosaic captures portrait and signature images to complement keyed variable data which is stored securely on the appropriate optical or magnetic media.

The benefits of NBS Mosaic include

- Permanent high quality colour image
- Database storage/retrieval of images and text
- Screen/Image verification
- Laser print hard copy image/data
- Interfaces to computerised time and attendance systems
- Continuous product support and training
- Systems tailored to suit customer requirements
- Variable image size/position
- Variable font selection
- Environmentally safe
- Simple menu driven operation
- Accurately reproduces varying skin tones
- Central or remote capture and issue
- Unequalled value for money
- Renders photo base systems obsolete
- Highest security card product

For further details contact Andrew Davidson
Telephone: 0932 351531   Fax: 0932 351382

APPLICATION CYCLE

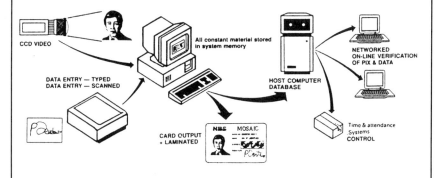

Total ID Solutions

178

- Transfer the risk:
    - pay an insurance company to take on the risk;
    - tell staff that they are responsible for their own personal property while at school.

- Minimise the risk:
    - take action which makes it more difficult for the criminal.

The usual answer is a combination of options, accepting whatever risk remains. It is important that every risk is judged against each option. Do not assume that nothing can be done or that an insurance policy covers everything.

Putting your plan into action

You are at the end of the planning phase and about to prepare for action. At this stage do not mistake enthusiasm for expertise. It is a common error of all bureaucracies that doing anything is better than appearing to be doing nothing, that producing a catalogue of 'initiatives' counts for more than spending time carefully preparing and implementing those initiatives. While the level of resources made available can be a measure of the importance attached to a problem, it does not necessarily indicate the success (or skill) with which it is tackled.

There must be some organisation within your school which will oversee the action. This could be an individual, such as the headteacher, or a small risk-management group made up from the governors, teaching and non-teaching staff. Reporting to this group will be individuals with specific areas of responsibility such as:

High-value equipment

Is portable high-value equipment locked away in secure stores each night? Who checks that this is done? Are rooms, like computer suites, secured each night? Is all equipment properly marked? Who is responsible for seeing this is done? Is there a regular audit of all high-value equipment?

Building security

How often are windows left open? Do you lock every internal door?

At last.

The school caretaker that never has a day off.

Telecom Security

Telecom Security, part of BT, can equip your school with an intruder alarm system which is connected through your phone line to our 24 hour monitoring station.

So the minute there's a problem, our operators will alert the police.

For a free survey or for further information, please return the coupon below or call us on 081-941 7561.

Because every school could do with a caretaker like Telecom Security.

☐ Please send me further information about how Telecom Security can help protect my premises.

☐ Please arrange for a free survey.

Name

Position

School

Telephone number (including STD code)

Address

Postcode

Please return coupon to: Gareth Britt, Telecom Security Ltd, FREEPOST TK 819, Hampton, Middlesex TW12 1BR. (No stamp is required.)

TELECOM SECURITY

BACKGROUND

Figures released by the Schools Minister Michael Fallon show that in the year from April 1989 to March 1990 there were 182,000 separate incidents of crime, 85,400 of vandalism in primary schools and 61,900 in secondary schools. Theft, arson and vandalism are dispiriting and morale-sapping for children, parents and teachers alike, all of whom contribute in different ways to the fabric of schools.

Security measures must be considered at every stage – from the very design of new schools to ensuring that all windows and doors are firmly locked each day.

ALARM SYSTEMS

Obviously, one of the most straightforward precautions is an alarm system. There are many different systems to choose from, and it is advisable to obtain specialist advice to ensure you invest in the type which will best suit your security problem. The Police Crime Prevention offices provide general advice on this topic.

INSTALLATION

A conventional bell-on-the-wall alarm can be sufficient. Like all alarms, these must be professionally installed and used correctly; the alternative means countless false alarms, wasting staff and police time for unnecessary call-outs. New legislation due to come into force in the London Boroughs in March 1992 allows for fines of up to £2000 for people whose alarms prove a nuisance.

CENTRAL MONITORING

Another consideration is a system linked to a central monitoring station staffed by the alarm company 24 hours a day.

One monitored system available on the market is provided by Telecom Security. This unique system offers intruder and vandalism protection 24 hours a day, 365 days a year, whether the school is staffed or not. Systems are specifically designed for the buildings in which they are to be used. A detailed survey reveals what is needed for your school's security and tells you why.

When a sensor is activated or a personal attack button pushed, the alarm system immediately transmits a signal through the telephone system to Telecom Security's central monitoring station. This station, the largest of its kind in Europe, is equipped with the most advanced computer and communications technology, enabling it to record special information about safety and security. The signal sent contains vital information which enables a trained operator to know exactly what type of emergency is occurring and alert the appropriate emergency services immediately.

In order to cut down on the number of false alarms being reported to the local emergency services, Telecom Security operators verify all incoming information – a unique safeguard in the system.

CONCLUSION

Alarm systems are a wise investment for schools since they can provide the protection required to deter the theft and vandalism that can rob us of valuable teaching time when incidents have to be investigated.

For further information ring 081 941 7561.

Why? Are filing cabinets locked? Why? What is your policy towards trespassers? What do you do to enforce it?

Good Neighbour Scheme

Remember that neighbours reporting crime to the police make themselves vulnerable to revenge attacks. This can scare willing volunteers into turning a blind eye.

The Good Neighbour Scheme avoids most of the problems associated with the traditional schoolwatch schemes but the neighbours must see the commitment the school have to making it work.

Junior Crime Prevention Panels

These are an important component of the educational element and can be a means of mobilising the children not only into keeping an eye on the school both during the day and at night but helping the local community – which could encourage them to help you.

Staff training

It is not enough to tell staff what they should be doing. They must know how to do it and why they are doing it if they are to develop a personal commitment. INSET time on security training might prove valuable.

Community use

Bringing the community into the school is one of the accepted methods of giving them a sense of sharing in the ownership of the building and encouraging them to protect it. But it can also bring its own problems. Opening part of the school might mean opening more than you need or letting anyone walk in and go where they like once an evening activity has begun. How can such issues be resolved at your school?

Visitors

Controlling visitors can be difficult. You should always be able to discover who is on the premises and why, but notices requesting all

visitors to report to the school office are often ignored. Challenges to visitors are frequently half-hearted. Have you considered giving each visitor a visitor tag and instructing staff that any stranger without a tag should be politely asked to go with them to the school office to get one? The children can help with this if they are told to inform a member of staff if they see a stranger without a tag.

Conclusion

If your school is experiencing relatively low levels of crime you may dismiss risk management as not worth the bother. This would be a mistake. Your school can, and will, suffer loss unless you do something to stop it.

Conversely, just because you are experiencing a spate of break-ins you should not concentrate on burglary to the exclusion of all other risks.

School crime is everyone's problem. The LEA, police and fire service are there to help. But unless you make it happen, nothing will be done.

Electronic Access Control

Ray Hilton

Access control in its simplest form is the locked door on a tool cupboard in the woodwork room, intended to keep the tools in and others out until the required time. *Electronic* access control boils down to the same thing: control of access to groups of people at various times to various places. This control is achieved by an electronically controlled 'beep' on the door lock that opens when the central unit says it can.

The simple way to achieve electronic access control is by the use of a key pad. When the correct code is entered, a relay will close which in turn energises the electric strike, allowing the door to be pushed open. It is usual to install a 'door-closer' to close the door after the person has gone through.

The main problem with this form of access control is that it is limited in the number of security codes and is usually a non-timed system. This means that any person knowing the code can gain entry 24 hours a day, seven days a week.

At the other end of the scale are the computer-based systems with facilities such as:

- control of up to 400 doors;

- selection of door/entry readers;

- selections of tokens to gain entry such as credit cards, proximity tags, encoded magnetic keys etc;

- considerable permutation of who goes where and when;

186

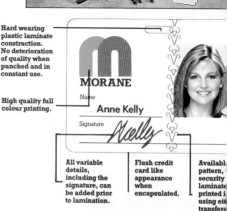

- print out of where people went;

- roll-call in case of fire so management can see who was where at a specific time;

- emergency opening of all doors.

Each site requires a system based on standard product but configured specifically for that installation.

A typical installation is the one at Essex University, comprising a central control system in the general administration office with remote control of the entrance doors for the accommodation blocks spread around the campus. The fire doors in the accommodation blocks are also monitored, and the means of entry is by a magnetically encoded key.

The central control allows a manager to set the times of entry to the accommodation areas. Holidays can be programmed in to prevent access, and lost keys can easily be removed from the system.

One major area to watch are doors and door hardware. If incorrectly fitted or of poor quality, breakdowns on the system will occur and the system will fail to inspire confidence.

Nowadays, the electronics of a system are very reliable; when the door and door hardware are correctly installed, the system will run very well.

The one on the left is easier to steal

The one on the right is protected with the 3M Tattle-Tape™ Library Security System, guaranteed in writing to give you at least an 80% reduction in losses in its first year.*

Our system offers the highest level of protection for several reasons - It guards all media. It's backed by 20 years experience in library security. And it features the 3M Tattle-Tape Security Strip; stringently controlled for quality, guaranteed for life, and made specifically for library use.

What's more we are so sure about its performance we give a 100% satisfaction guarantee.*

To learn more, call 3M Library Security Systems, the global leader in library security: 061-237 6151. And make your library stock harder to lift than a 3,000lb car.

* See your 3M sales consultant for details and additional terms of 3M's 80% Loss Reduction and 100% Satisfaction Guarantees.

Innovation working for you™

3M

3M and Tattle-Tape are trademarks.

6.8

Library Security

Tony Wilcox

Case study: Garth Hill Comprehensive

'Since we installed a library security system, book losses have been virtually non-existent,' according to Jackie Wells, library assistant at Garth Hill School in Bracknell, Berkshire.

Garth Hill, a 1000-pupil comprehensive, amalgamated three smaller libraries in June 1987 to form a single large collection. With a stock of around 10,000 items, the library is managed by a school librarian cum English teacher and her full-time assistant. Pupil librarians come in on a rota system to staff the desk and to learn how the library works.

Fully staffed, well stocked and efficiently run, Garth Hill School library has become something of a showpiece. But this was not always the case. 'Before we installed a security system, our book losses were phenomenal,' says Val Taylor the school's librarian. 'When we came to combine the three existing libraries, we discovered that we'd lost at least 25 per cent of our stock over the years. There'd been no proper security at all, and we'd simply lost track of the books'.

The new library was a major undertaking for the school, so an effective means of protecting that investment was considered essential right from the start. The school chose a technically advanced library security system, consisting of two basic elements. The first is a 'trigger' device, easily fitted into each item, whether hardback, paperback or magazine. Concealed within the book, the trigger is virtually undetectable to library users.

The second element is a free-standing sensing unit at the library exit. Books are sensitised, usually using a small hand-held unit, and remain so until desensitised at the issue desk by library staff. If a student attempts to steal, or forgetfully walks off with, a book that has not been desensitised, the trigger sets off an alarm within the sensing unit which alerts the library staff. Books cannot be shielded from detection by bags, clothing or the human body.

According to Val Taylor: 'All our new stock is triggered, even magazines, which used to disappear very quickly, sometimes on the day they arrived! Now, because we don't have to spend money on replacing stolen items, all our budget goes on new stock.'

Costs and savings

The hidden cost to libraries of unchecked pilfering is startlingly high. Average losses are estimated to be somewhere betwen 1 and

3 per cent for old stock, rising dramatically to around 20 or 30 per cent for more attractive new stock.

Whitaker's put the average price of a new, non fiction, hardback in 1991 at £25.60, and the average fiction paperback at £4.38. A quick calculation reveals that thousands of pounds worth of stock can walk out of libraries every year, unless effective security is introduced. The cost of getting a library security system up and running is usually less than £5,000. Assuming a typical 90 per cent reduction in book losses, such a system can pay for itself within two years.

Savings are not the only benefit

As schools and colleges take greater responsibility for managing their own budgets, awareness is growing of the need for efficient resource management. Whatever its size, the library represents one of the school's most valuable assets, taking up a large proportion of its annual expenditure. Many school and college libraries have diversified into larger resource centres, with a wide range of audio and video materials, as well as books. A good library security system uses the same simple method to protect books, records, cassettes, CDs and computer diskettes.

Although cost savings may be the deciding factor in the purchase of a library security system, they are by no means the only benefit. Many school and college librarians say that their libraries have become more attractive and important to users since the installation of a security system. Issues and requests have increased, and books can be traced without the frustration and time-wasting caused by the fruitless search for stolen items. Being able to provide a better service improves staff confidence and morale, enabling them to display new stock without fear of loss.

A modern library security system gives better protection than alternative methods, such as hidden cameras or window locks, and avoids unpleasant confrontations arising from individual bag or clothing searches. It can also eliminate the inconvenience to students of leaving bags and coats outside the library. Librarians are free to get on with their work, instead of keeping a watchful eye on borrowers.

Closed-circuit Television*

Closed-circuit television (CCTV) surveillance systems are in widespread use as a means of conveying visual information from a selected location back to a monitoring position. CCTV is relatively new as a means of protecting schools, but rapidly proving its worth.

Systems vary considerably in size and complexity, according to the application in hand. However, in its simplest form, the basic system would comprise:

- a camera, fitted with suitable lens to survey the scene in question;

- a communication link between the camera and monitoring location;

- a monitor to display the camera's information in the form of an image of the scene.

Security applications in schools range from a single camera system which monitors a specific vulnerable area, to multiple camera systems providing comprehensive surveillance of large, complex sites.

Cameras

A range of monochrome cameras is available to suit the widely varying conditions encountered in different environments.

Cameras fall into four broad categories:

---

* This article has been adapted from a booklet produced by the North East Regional Schools Security Group entitled *Security in Schools – a Management Guide*.

CamEra

CLOSED CIRCUIT TELEVISION CAN COVER:

SWIMMING POOLS, ENTRANCES, CORRIDORS, LABORATORIES, COMPUTER ROOMS, STAFF SAFETY, MUSIC ROOMS, CAFETERIAS, SCHOOL SHOPS, DORMITORIES, ENTRANCES, LIBRARIES, FIRST AID STATIONS, PLAYGROUND AREAS, GYMS, FOR SECURITY COMMUNICATION, HEALTH AND SAFETY AND PEACE OF MIND. WITH EXTERNAL PROTECTION AGAINST VANDALISM, WE COULD EVEN COVER THE "BACK OF THE BIKE SHEDS ! "

0800 577 577

CALL FREE ON THE ABOVE NUMBER FOR A NO COST DISCUSSION WITH ONE OF OUR LOCAL CONSULTANTS.

- general purpose;
- low light;
- very low light;
- solid-state.

General purpose cameras

These are normally fitted with a 'vidicon' tube and operate well in environments with a high level of light, either controlled or natural. They are better for internal applications as the cameras do not handle changing light levels very well. The required amount of light is quantified as being greater than 5 lux (equivalent externally to typical side-street lighting in a town).

Low light cameras

Ideally suited to both indoor and outdoor locations, these cameras are typically fitted with a 'newvicon' tube and are sensitive to low levels of natural and artificial light. Because of their extra-sensitivity they will be equipped with an 'auto-iris lens', which controls the amount of light entering the camera under rapidly changing lighting conditions.

The operating light levels are in the order of 0.5 lux (bright moonlight) or lower. A variation on this camera is the 'extended red newvicon' tube. By mounting infra-red emitting lamps adjacent to the camera, the night-viewing capability of the camera is considerably improved.

Very low light cameras

A range of cameras with special tubes exists for those applications where moonlight or starlight are the only available light sources. These cameras are known as SIT (silicon intensified target) and are extremely sensitive, amplifying any available light. As a result, they are expensive but ideally suited to high-risk night-time security applications.

Solid-state cameras

Often referred to as CCD (charge-coupled device) cameras, these

cameras have no tubes and are consequently smaller in size and require less maintenance than tube cameras. They operate at low light levels and are priced competitively against tube cameras.

Technically, there is still a limitation with the 'resolution' of CCD cameras: a slight lack of definition in low light; however, the CCD camera does not suffer the drawbacks of a tube camera, such as 'burn' and 'distortion'.

Fixed lenses

The lens is the 'eye' of the camera, conveying visual information in the form of light to the camera tube. The lens may be a simple 'fixed' lens, focussed on a scene, with no further refinements. The fixed lens may also be equipped with a controlled iris for tube protection in varying light levels.

The 'focal length' of the lens will be selected to give the desired wide or narrow field of view. Short focal lengths will offer wider views of the scene in question.

Large focal lengths will have the effect of bringing distant areas of the scene closer to the viewer, ie, a small part of the scene is 'blown up' to fill the monitor screen.

Fixed lenses are the most economical solution to situations requiring general surveillance, such as schools.

Site evaluation

Selection of the correct version of camera and lens will depend upon information gathered on site, particularly in respect of the required area of coverage, the lighting levels and other environmental operating conditions.

Area of coverage

The distance the camera has to 'see', and the desired amount of detail at the maximum distance, will have a bearing on the camera type and position, and on the type of lens fitted.

PRINCES
CATERING PRODUCTS

A COMPREHENSIVE RANGE
OF QUALITY PRODUCTS FOR ALL YOUR CATERING NEEDS

Princes Catering Products
Royal Liver Buildings Liverpool L3 1NX Tel. 051 236 9282

Clearly, an increase in the angle of view is gained at the expense of image size. For a particularly wide area of surveillance it may be necessary to use two cameras, each with lenses of moderate focal length, to ensure reasonable image definition.

Lighting levels

The quality and intensity of natural ambient light, and any additional artificial light (spotlight, street lamps etc). should be carefully studied to establish the type of camera required. The chosen camera may be assisted by fitting infra-red lamps to enhance picture quality.

The position and intensity of any highlights in the scene, such as sunlight, headlamps, spotlight etc, would have a bearing on the type of camera and its viewing position.

A tube camera may perform adversely under various lighting conditions. A solid-state camera may prove a better choice under these conditions.

Camera assembly

The environment will dictate the type of housing required, and additional control functions necessary. For example, an outdoor camera in an exposed location would require a weatherproof housing, with internal heater for low temperatures, and possibly a wiper and/or washer fitted for ease of cleaning.

Camera mounting

Various methods of supporting the camera assembly are available, providing stability and efficiency in wind and storm conditions.

Mounts are available for fixing to wall, ceiling, pedestal, pole or tower, depending upon the application. Where a pole or tower assembly is used, anti-climb protection is required, often in the form of non-drying paint or metal outriggers.

Video and control signal transmission

The methods used to transmit the video and control signals between camera and control position will vary according to the geography, size and location of the site in question. With multiple signal equipment, the same cable will be used for both video and control signals.

Coaxial cable

The normal method used for school applications is to interconnect system components using coaxial cable. This is limited mainly by the distance required for the communication link, with the performance beginning to deteriorate between 300 and 600 metres, depending upon the grade of cable used.

Twisted pair cable

Twisted pair cable involves the use of transmitting and receiving equipment and allows transmission of signals over long distances.

This wiring method may be better suited to a large site, where coaxial cable would have distance limitations.

Wireless signal communication

For applications where 'hard-wiring' is impractical or undesirable, it is now possible to convert the camera signals into other forms of energy for transmission through air.

This would avoid running cables between buildings, by overhead catenaries or underground burial.

Control and recording equipment

Video multiplexer

A typical video multiplexer takes the incoming signals from up to 16 remote cameras, and displays them simultaneously on a monitor in a permutation of full size and compressed pictures.

The multiplexer has the added advantage that all cameras connected to it may be simultaneously recorded on a single magnetic tape by using a video cassette recorder (VCR). This ensures that no camera activity is missed during recording, and playback of recorded scenes is presented in an easily viewed format.

Video recording

Camera scenes may be recorded onto magnetic tape in various formats to enable playback of scenes. The recorded information may be 'stamped' with the time and date to assist in submission of the recorded material as evidence in any legal proceedings.

The standard two-hour video cassette may be extended to cover up to a 72-hour period (useful for weekend recording) by capturing selected camera information at preset intervals. Alternatively, the cassette may be changed daily or twice daily, as required.

The unit may be programmed to capture the continuous image from a particular camera during an alarm incident.

Usually, a number of cassettes are used which are sufficient for a full week's recording, and these are re-recorded each subsequent week unless an incident has occurred, in which case the relevant cassette will be removed from use.

6.10

Managing Resources

Jim Donnelly

All resources – staff, books, stationery – in a school need to be managed, but here we are dealing specifically with the management of expensive items of hardware. We shall look first at such things as computers, video recorders, video cameras, and lathes, which may be used by one or more departments; then we will consider photocopiers which bring their own particular management problems.

In the past it was usual for LEA advisers to provide the money for large items such as lathes, but under LMS schools have to make their own provision. This coincides with the wider use and availability of computer- and video-based technologies. There is thus a need for schools to have a clear policy on resource allocation, purchase, repair/maintenance and ultimate replacement. One can represent this diagrammatically as in Figure 6.10.1.

The school policy should cover all four areas. It is useful to look at each in turn.

Allocation

There is undoubtedly much pressure on schools to live 'from hand to mouth', especially where the provision of an annual allocation for hardware may lead to redundancies among teaching staff. The management issue here may revolve around providing the maximum number of teachers with minimal resources or fewer teachers

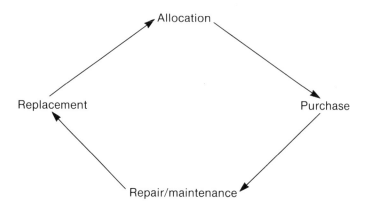

Figure 6.10.1 *The cycle of funds for hardware*

with better resources. Each school must make its own decision in its own particular circumstances.

It is advisable to include all funding (see Table 6.10.1) in one 'pool', otherwise some departments may be getting more than their fair share; for example, Science may be a more attractive proposition for gifts than, say, History. The senior management in school must ensure that all sources are considered together, since ultimately the students suffer if some subjects are better resourced than others.

School's annual budget share.

LEA grants – usually limited to Government-supported initiatives.

TVEI money – if you have not already had yours!

PTAs – who may supply the funds for so-called 'extras'.

Charities – usually very specific and often not for hardware.

Local industry – often have spare equipment (which can now be 'written-off' against tax) but who are not likely to be able to provide much in the way of new equipment.

Table 6.10.1 *Possible sources of funding*

Once the total amount for hardware is known, priorities need to be set. There are some questions which need to be asked:

1. Will each department have an annual share or will they take it in turns to have allocations?

2. Will all hardware items be school-owned (encouraging whole-school thinking) or departmentally-owned (possibly encouraging more careful use)?

3. Will departments be encouraged to put in joint bids?

4. Who will arbitrate on bids?

Even when one has used this procedure, there does need to be some flexibility in case special offers appear which have a time limit on them. A recent example has been the funding of CD-ROM purchases through a DES grant which required immediate action by schools. Such decisions are made easier if the policy looks at purchasing over at least a three-year period.

Purchase

Schools are now more aware that careful buying can make even a fairly modest sum of money go much further. Value for money does not necessarily mean buying the cheapest but equally paying more does not always mean that you get more. Now that LEA central purchasing organisations are more customer- (ie school-) orientated, they have two useful functions. First, they can often arrange bulk-purchase discounts. Second, they can often provide sound advice, which helps schools avoid the worst disasters when

---

1. Is the manufacturer reputable and reliable?

2. Are spares easily obtained at a reasonable price?

3. Does the supplier have a good reputation for after-sales service?

4. Is servicing provided on-site or do you have to send the item off by post (at the school's expense)?

5. Do you need quick servicing (eg same day) or can you wait several weeks for the item to be repaired?

6. How long does the guarantee last for? Does it include labour and parts? Are there any exclusions?

7. Can you get a discount for buying more than one? If so, are any other local schools willing to join with you to get it?

Table 6.10.2 *Questions to ask before purchasing equipment*

they are desperately trying to get as much as they can for a small amount of money. Table 6.10.2 lists some basic questions which can help the decision-making process.

A special word needs to be added about contracts. The legal term which should be printed on your mind before you sign any order is *caveat emptor*: this translates as the familiar term, 'let the buyer beware'. If you sign a contract the school will be kept to it. In the past, LEAs often took the responsibility for ensuring that such contracts did not contain any hidden conditions which would operate against them: and if they did make mistakes, the LEA funded them. Under LMS, when the school buys something it bears the responsibility for ensuring that the small print does not contain any 'hidden extras'!

The other thing which often did not concern schools but which does now is whether to buy, rent or lease equipment. There are several advantages in leasing or renting:

1.   The cost can be spread over several years.

2.   Equipment can sometimes be updated more easily (provided that one takes the new equipment from the present supplier).

3.   If the school gets a badly-made item, it does not suffer the full cost of trying to put it right.

The advantages of buying are:

1.   It is cheaper in the long run, unless one has to spend a lot on repairs.

2.   If there is a long-term budget plan, it should be possible to update items.

3.   The rental cost cannot be raised. (Not all rental agreements allow for an increase in annual payments but some do.)

4.   You are more likely to be able to cover the item with luminous security paint and the like.

One has to be very careful to read the small print in rental agreements, as some of them tie the school in to the company for a long period of time unless the company chooses to waive the terms; the latter is only likely if you agree to take new equipment from them.

1. Do we need it now? If so, have we got the money to buy it?
2. Is it likely to be reliable?
3. Is there the option of an extended guarantee at an affordable cost?
4. What is the total cost over its likely life, including repairs and maintenance?
5. Are there going to be major advances in the technology over the next few years?

Table 6.10.3 *To rent/lease or buy?*

It is interesting to note that renting televisions was more popular when sets were not as reliable as they are today, since rental agreements included the cost of repairs. If you purchase a television nowadays, you will get at least a year's guarantee, with the option of a further guarantee period for an extra payment. Washing machines, on the other hand, are often rented by schools because, for some reason or other, they are not as reliable as some other items of equipment. The answer to the question, 'Should we rent/lease or buy?' is therefore likely to be different depending on the item to be purchased. Some questions to help make the decision are given in Table 6.10.3.

Once the equipment has been obtained, the next thing which needs to be planned is how to fund its repair/maintenance.

Repair/maintenance

If the equipment has been rented or leased, it is usual for the cost to include routine maintenance and repair. However, you should *check the small print* to ensure that the cover is as all-embracing as you think it is. There may, for example, be clauses which involve the school in paying the cost of parts which are damaged through negligence.

If the equipment has been purchased, provision needs to be made for its maintenance and for possible repairs. Some schools keep a special budget for all maintenance while others make separate provision for each expensive item. It has to be decided whether the school will pay for the repair of departmental equipment or whether departments will have to fund it themselves.

Replacement

A point in the life of most equipment is reached – particularly with computers and video recorders – where it becomes uneconomic to continue to repair it. Decisions have to be taken about when such a point has been reached. Who decides? Who pays for the replacement? What is done with the old equipment?

An important point to bear in mind is that if a lot of equipment is bought at one time (for example, with TVEI funding) it will need to be replaced at about the same time. This is a good reason for having a clear replacement policy stretching over at least a three-year period.

Photocopiers

The general rules which apply to the purchase of video recorders and the like also apply to photocopiers. However, there are additional points which need to be borne in mind when one is considering this particular piece of equipment. Whether one buys or rents/leases a photocopier, it is usual for an additional maintenance charge to be payable. The normal way in which this is charged is a fraction of a penny (say 0.7p) per copy done. This works on the basis that the more the machine is used, the more time it will cost the company providing it.

The first thing to bear in mind is that, while there is not much apparent difference between, say, 0.7p and 0.8p, the difference is in reality quite large (£400 per year) when one is doing maybe 400,000 copies a year. A further complication is that if one begins to charge departments for copies they may do fewer than they did when they were not charged.

---

1. The rental/lease charge per year (if applicable).
2. The copy cost.
3. The paper cost (popularly but erroneously believed to be the most significant cost element in photocopying).
4. The likely number of copies per year – but watch for variations.

Table 6.10.4 *Costs of a photocopier*

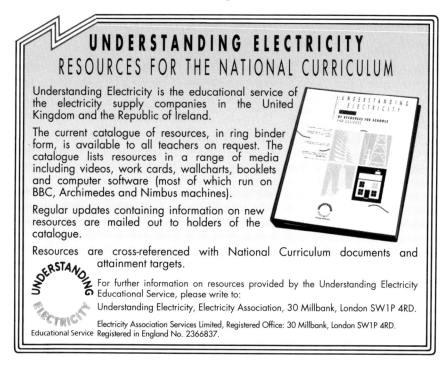

UNDERSTANDING ELECTRICITY
RESOURCES FOR THE NATIONAL CURRICULUM

Understanding Electricity is the educational service of the electricity supply companies in the United Kingdom and the Republic of Ireland.

The current catalogue of resources, in ring binder form, is available to all teachers on request. The catalogue lists resources in a range of media including videos, work cards, wallcharts, booklets and computer software (most of which run on BBC, Archimedes and Nimbus machines).

Regular updates containing information on new resources are mailed out to holders of the catalogue.

Resources are cross-referenced with National Curriculum documents and attainment targets.

For further information on resources provided by the Understanding Electricity Educational Service, please write to:

Understanding Electricity, Electricity Association, 30 Millbank, London SW1P 4RD.

Electricity Association Services Limited, Registered Office: 30 Millbank, London SW1P 4RD. Educational Service Registered in England No. 2366837.

The best way to deal with this is to establish the costs (see Table 6.10.4). If you want to be able to manage these costs, it may be advisable to pay fixed costs centrally, with departments paying for the paper and copy charges. This should mean that the copier account balances at the end of the year. (This is not possible if you have an agreement which allows so many 'free' copies per month. This arrangement is usually not suitable for schools, which have peaks (eg examination times) and troughs (eg August) in demand for photocopying.)

Another management issue is access to the copier, which can arouse much emotion in schools. Whatever the decision of the school it is important that all aspects are considered and that the reasons for the policy are clear to all staff. While there are good reasons why copying should be done *for* teaching staff as opposed to *by* them, it needs to be clear that this is not because they are not trusted: the facility to use the photocopier can be seen as a status symbol if one is not careful.

Choosing a Desktop Laser Printer*

Introduction

There are over 50 brands of laser printers on the UK market, most offering features which appear to be very similar. It's not until you look a little closer at the different features and how those capabilities can offer user benefits that the choice of desktop laser printer becomes clearer, and a lot easier.

For example, the problem with a personal laser printer is that it has been designed to be just that. Try connecting two or three different PCs to it and you'll probably find that each user has to configure the printer manually to their own emulation or format requirements before printing.

This article has been written to provide a useful checklist against which to compare equipment features for current and future needs.

Connecting A Laser Printer: The Basics

Emulations

Before you can start printing, your printer and software have to be able to work together. PC printers include one or more sets of printer control commands, known as a printer control language, or printer emulation.

---

* This article has been adapted from a booklet produced by Rank Xerox entitled *Choosing a Laser Printer for the Corporate Environment.*

No matter how hard these four PCs work, they'll never see a hold up.

The machine you see sitting on the bench before you is the Xerox 4030 laser printer.

Although it's one of our smaller printers, it will never stop the PCs behind it for speeding or even leaving their stations.

Because not only can it cope with virtually any PC software programme but it's almost 40% faster than the market leader.

We believe it's the perfect printer for a whole department and by far the best machine in its class.

But don't just take our word for it. 'Which Computer?' reached the same conclusions in their August 1990 issue.

Of course the  Xerox 4030 is only one of a range of printers we make, all of which have similarly impeccable credentials. And all with

one other quite unique feature.

A machine replacement, total satisfaction, three year, no quibble guarantee that comes as part of our service agreement.

If you'd like to know how our printers are guaranteed to

stop your business slowing down talk to Kim McTier.

And she will arrange for someone to come and present you with the evidence.

Call 0800 010 766, or write:

FREEPOST 2, Uxbridge UB8 1BR.

RANK XEROX
The Document Company

With software packages, and among laser printers, Hewlett-Packard's Printer Control Language, (HP-PCL), has been universally adopted as a *de facto* standard.

By ensuring that the laser printer you purchase is 'LaserJet Series II-compatible', you can be assured of the widest possible compatibility between your application software and your laser printer.

Interfaces

Personal computers normally provide two interfaces for the purposes of connecting output devices such as printers: parallel and serial. They may be labelled as such on the computer, or alternatively as LPT (parallel), or COM (serial).

Parallel interfaces are generally faster than serial interfaces, both in use, and when setting up the printer. They are also far easier to set up.

A serial interface can be a distinct advantage when the physical siting of the printer and computer demands a connecting cable longer than a couple of metres.

You should always ensure a printer can accept extra interfaces, even if you only need parallel to start with.

Speed

The actual speed of a laser printer depends to a great extent on the type of output. Simple text, using the printer's resident fonts is fastest. Complex full page graphics with text increase the processing time. The degree of sophistication offered by the printer driver in your applications software has a bearing on the printer speed too.

Fonts

Laser printers are supplied with a limited set of bit-mapped fonts stored in permanent memory. These should include both Portrait and Landscape fonts for convenience. With a condensed Landscape font, you can print a wide spreadsheet report across the length of a sheet of paper.

The printer should support additional fonts by means of font cartridges, or downloaded fonts.

Printers with two font cartridge slots available cut down on the hassle of having to change cartridges to accommodate differing user

The Dataproducts LZR 960 – The Copywriter's Dream

"There was really no question of which of the 16 PostScript printers was the best value. For less than £2000, the Dataproducts LZR 960 provides everything the other printers do *and* Adobe Level 2 PostScript. There was some debate over whether it could be reasonably compared with other printers in this review, being the only one with Level 2 compatibility. But at the end of the test, the Dataproducts had beaten its competitors fairly and squarely. On a combination of speed, quality, convenience, potential and price, the LZR 960 was awarded the PCW Seal of Approval."

Personal Computer World, December 1991

"The Dataproducts LZR 960 is an attractive high-level choice."

PC Magazine, November 1991

"... several PostScript Level 1 images that I've previously timed on Level 1 printers were dramatically quicker on the 9 page per minute LZR 960."
Awarded ☆ ☆ ☆ ☆ ☆

Apple Business, December 1991

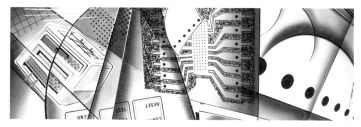

"... you are unlikely to regret an early move to PostScript Level 2."
Awarded four and half mice (out of five)

MacUser, 1 November 1991

"Clear performance gains will be achieved by moving to the LZR 960."

PC User, Issue 172, 20 November 1991

With reviews this good, who needs advertising copy?

And it's not just in the UK that the LZR 960 from Dataproducts has received such widespread acclaim. In benchmark tests carried out by MacWeek in the US, the LZR 960 outperformed not only the Apple LaserWriter II NT and NTX, but also the new IIf and IIg.

PostScript Level 2 is the next major development in printer technology. Don't buy yesterday's PostScript printer when you can have tomorrow's Level 2 technology today.

Buy the Dataproducts LZR 960 and invest in the future.

FAST FACTS 1

For further information on the LZR 960 and supplies, call Dataproducts on 0734 884777
Dataproducts UK Ltd., Unit 1, Heron Industrial Estate, Spencers Wood, Reading, Berkshire RG7 1PJ
PostScript is a registered trademark of Adobe Systems Incorporated.

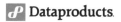
Dataproducts

requirements. The larger the capacity of the cartridge, the more fonts can be readily available to the user.

Setup procedure

The font panel display must include a means of altering the basic default characteristics, such as paper type, emulation, or font. It should also have a means of communicating the current status, and any warning, or error messages.

The system for altering defaults should follow a simple menu style, and be easy to use without having to resort to a handbook each time. The display should include messages rather than codes for the same reason.

When a laser printer stops working, it's nice to see a message that says 'Toner empty', rather than a cryptic code that sends the operator off to search for the manual.

Software control

Control of most of the printer's functions directly from the user's PC, rather than a printer front panel, is helpful when using a mix of applications software requiring different printer emulations. Life is a lot easier if the printer can 'soft-switch' between emulations. This is particularly important for printers which will be put to use as a shared resource.

Paper and other consumables

Paper handling

The capacity of the paper tray, in sheets, is important. Basically, the bigger the better, especially when the printer is used as a shared resource. A low paper-tray capacity increases stoppages for refills, and leads to incomplete printouts.

Dual paper bins

Dual paper bins increase the unattended capacity of the printer. Even more useful, combined with a printer that can switch between paper bins under software control, you can use both letter-headed paper and plain sheets without having to resort to manual paper feed.

For mail-merge operations, the advantages of a dual-bin printer which can print the first page on letter-head, and follow up with continuation sheets, or envelopes, from the second bin, are enough to make a dual-bin printer the only type you should consider.

Materials

Laser printers are not restricted to printing on sheets of cut paper. They must also print on transparencies, adhesive labels, envelopes, and thin card stock.

All of these require the printer to support manual feed input. In the case of envelopes, the paper tray may double as a feed tray for limited automatic feeding.

Consumables

Besides paper refills, a laser printer occasionally needs to have its toner and developer cartridges renewed. Normal manufacturers' practice is to give figures for the life of these consumables in the number of pages that can be printed at a specified density.

Usually, the density quoted is 5 per cent. This seems low until you realise that a page full of lower-case 'k' characters will be an approximate density of 25 per cent. Of course, any increase of density over the quoted figure will reduce the number of pages that may be printed per toner or developer cartridge.

Maintenance and support

Vendor support

With laser printers, it is usual for manufacturers to offer a 12-month warranty. The important point to consider is whether that warranty covers service 'on-site', or whether it requires the printer to be returned to the manufacturer for warranty repair. Obviously it is faster, cheaper and more convenient to the user for repairs to be made on-site.

The vast majority of laser printer manufacturers offer a 12-month on-site maintenance contract within the purchase price of the machine. If the expected usage comes close to the duty cycle of the machine it is worthwhile purchasing an extended maintenance contract to cover the next two to three years.

Duty cycle

The duty cycle of a laser printer is usually specified as the number of pages that can be produced per month. This is not a limit on the actual number of pages but an expression of the printer's life expectancy. Exceeding the duty cycle will not necessarily harm the printer, but it will reduce the lifespan of the print engine over an extended period.

Footprint

The 'footprint' of a laser printer is the area covered by paper trays, or sheet guides, as well as that of the printer itself. Paper trays which are fully housed within the main body of the printer are least likely to cause space problems, or suffer from being accidentally bumped into.

Memory

The standard issue memory size tends to be 512Kb, which is adequate for most word processing tasks, and simple graphics such as spreadsheet graphs.

The ability to add extra memory is important. A full page of graphics at 300dpi requires at least 1Mb of memory, before taking into account any forms overlays or additional fonts you may want to download.

In shared environments, where additional users may each wish to download fonts, at least 4Mb of memory may be required.

Using a laser printer as a shared resource

Software control

User control from the PC, either through application software or directly, is vital to effective unattended use. If each different application, or user, needs a different emulation, you'll readily appreciate the convenience of being able to switch emulations without having to walk over to the printer.

Printer sharing devices

Apart from adding it to a local area network, there are many other ways of sharing a printer – from simple mechanical switches, through to intelligent printer sharers.

Mechanical switches may be considered better value for money depending upon the application, but have the undesirable effect of locking everyone else out, even after the job is finished.

An intelligent printer sharer will be able to support several users transparently. By incorporating setup strings, the intelligent printer sharer can enable a single printer to present itself as, say, a LaserJet-compatible to one user, while offering an Epson emulation to another.

This allows all users to use their favourite software without re-configuration. In order for this to happen, the printer must offer software control of most of its features, and the printer sharing device needs sufficient memory to receive incoming jobs while printing the current job.

Auto paper eject

If a printer only prints the last page of a document when forced to by the arrival of the following document, it is possible for pages to go missing, especially in a busy office.

The usual way to avoid this is to set the printer to eject a completed page within a set time. Unfortunately, this can cause pages containing complex graphics to be ejected before they are completed.

To overcome this problem, a shared printer should be able to accept software control of the time that a printer will wait before ejecting a page.

Speed

Personal printers are rated at four to six pages per minute. Shared printers should be rated at eight pages per minute minimum for small workgroups, or clusters of PCs. For more intensive use, a rated speed of at least ten pages per minute is essential.

Shared printers are intensively-used. A fast printer won't keep users hanging around waiting for their jobs to complete printing.

WE CAN TEACH YOU A THING OR 2 ABOUT SCHOOL CLEANING

It's a question of understanding the individual needs. Understanding the problems. Knowing the solutions. Being able to provide the right sort of local service at the right sort of price. Whether it's one school or a number of different locations, our experience means that you can leave it to us.

Call us. You may learn something.

INITIAL

Initial Contract Services
Initial House
81 High Street
Potters Bar
Herts EN6 5LW
Tel: 0707 44541

A BET COMPANY

IN A CLASS OF ITS OWN!

222

Contract Cleaning and Catering

Jim Donnelly

The delegation of cleaning and catering has caused more than a few problems for schools, already trying hard to come to terms with other aspects of LMS.

Compulsory competitive tendering

These difficulties are in part due to the Government's insistence that cleaning, for example, should be the subject of compulsory competitive tendering. The principle is sound enough but it was thrust upon schools which were not used to managing cleaning, except in a fairly informal way. In many cases LEAs were anxious to maintain the service they offered – and preserve the jobs of their employees – and therefore they tendered for the contract.

It is probably fair to say that it has taken some time for the initial problems of moving from the old system to the new to be ironed out. For many schools the short-term impact was felt in a sharp fall in cleaning standards. Some bids were unrealistic – both from LEAs and from private contractors who were anxious to get a foot in the school door – and those who suffered were the staff and pupils in schools.

Keeping to the contract

As the dust settles, schools are beginning to realise that the contract for cleaning is similar in many ways to any other contract. The following advice may help in putting this particular part of LMS into some kind of perspective.

1. Read the contract carefully. Ensure that the cleaning to be done is clearly set out and is in keeping with the school's priorities. If you feel the school's priorities have changed, try to negotiate a change in the contract.
2. Remember that you are paying for the service. Identify who the contractor's representative is and make sure that any complaints about cleaning standards are specific, detailed and written. Have a system whereby teaching staff and the caretaker can pass on comments to the member of the senior management team who is responsible for dealing with the contractor.
3. Plan ahead for Parents' Evenings and the like which may require a variation to the contract, and make sure that the required notice is given.
4. Remember that staff absence among the cleaning staff is not for you to sort out: the contractor should do this.
5. The final point is in many ways the most important one: the school needs a policy on how important cleanliness is and how much it is prepared to pay for it. Remember that an improvement in standards – assuming that the contract is being honoured – may have to be paid for. Under a delegated budget, the implications for staffing and resources in other areas are clear.

Some of these points are more difficult to resolve in the short term, especially if the contract you are working with is not a realistic one. However, over time, as the school gains more control, there is the opportunity to set cleaning standards and to get value for money in this area.

Catering

The pattern of provision of school meals varies considerably from one end of the country to the other. Some LEAs have abandoned the provision of more than a token meals' service. Where they have not, the same principles should be applied to the operation of the contract for catering (whether the LEA holds the contract or not) as to the cleaning contract. There are two important points which are specific to school meals. First, if they are not provided efficiently they may overrun the lunch-hour. If this happens, make sure that you complain to the contractor until an improvement is affected. Second, you may feel that the standard and/or suitability of the food provided is not satisfactory.

Quality is a subjective judgement, unlike the length of time taken to serve meals, which can be readily measured. In this area, you are well advised to involve the students and their parents if necessary if you feel unhappy about what is being offered. In the final analysis, it is they who pay (either directly or indirectly) for the food.

The future

Contracts such as those mentioned above were put out under

compulsory competitive tendering as one service, to be provided by one contractor. As LMS gradually matures, however, schools are likely to have more freedom to negotiate their own contracts for cleaning, catering and grounds maintenance. Add to this the fact that schools may wish in future to contract out some secretarial work and/or maintenance of the buildings, and soon one can see that schools will have a multitude of contracts with perhaps a multitude of people.

There is a view that when that happens, schools may well decide to opt for what are called *multi-service* contracts, where all such services are contracted to one contractor: this is beginning to sound a bit like the situation which existed when LEAs had control of schools! However, the difference will be that schools control the budget and therefore the contractor will have to be responsive to their clients' needs.

6.13

Management of Capital Works – Opportunities for Growth

Jim Crooks

Introduction

Capital works projects need to be well planned and managed. Successful projects can be described as those which:

- represent good value for money (immediate and long term);

- are flexible to cope with changes (demographic, technological, etc);

- make full use of all opportunities available;

- are part of long-term plans and objectives.

Capital works management is a relatively new area of opportunity to many managers involved in the education sector, where the management of capital works projects has been recently devolved from central control.

This paper sets out some of the strategic factors affecting capital works management together with some examples to demonstrate their importance.

In the conclusion, we have made some recommendations about when, how and from whom education executives should seek assistance.

Background

Vast new opportunities are open to those managing our education establishments. The successful managers will provide high-quality, efficient services by making full use of all the opportunities open to them.

Among such opportunities is the freedom to control their own capital works programmes: the opportunity to match programmes to specific requirements and the opportunity to raise finance by introducing flexibility into the capital programmes in order to raise additional revenue and contribute more to the community.

The management of capital works is part of a total business plan which includes running, maintenance and replacement costs. While this article will refer to buildings and infrastructure as an example of capital works, similar principles apply to any other capital element.

In referring to building works we include extensions, refurbishment, alterations, conversions and new buildings. Maintenance will be referred to as it affects choices between capital schemes.

The following sections refer to some of the strategic issues associated with capital works management together with examples of their effect on the success of capital works projects.

Function and flexibility

The principal functions of any educational establishment are simple to set down. However, secondary and tertiary issues may be more difficult both to identify and to mutually reconcile. A simple list of all the functions and requirements is essential.

Flexibility is one such requirement. It must take account of the expected short-, medium- and long-term requirements while leaving a margin for the unexpected.

Short-term flexibility is the ability to change uses on a day-to-day basis, such as the movement of furniture and loose equipment; medium-term could be changes on a term-by-term basis, such as the exchange of a language laboratory for a music room; long-term could be the ability to change from form rooms to lecture theatres and seminar rooms.

Function can also take account of alternative uses – both those

Accommodation solutions for schools

Thinking Cap!

Building is a science that Bovis has studied on an international scale, seeking the quickest, the most economic and practical solutions to all manner of projects, all over the world.

The lessons learned in 100 years of construction are applied today across all aspects of every contract for clients ranging from large developers to local authorities.

In the educational sector Bovis has completed projects throughout the UK and USA and even in Japan, where we are construction advisers for the Kobe Institute, founded by St Catherine's College, Oxford. And, for those who have more on their minds than new building, our management-led methods of contracting will invariably help to save time and money, without sacrificing care or quality.

If you want to know more about our academic approach to building contact,

Paul Coxon

Bovis Construction Ltd

Bovis House, Northolt Road, Harrow,

Middlesex HA2 0EE.   Tel: 081-422 3488

which earn revenue for the establishment and those which benefit and enrich the whole community. Early consideration of function and the degree of flexibility is essential if the objectives are to be met at minimum, or even no, cost.

For example, it may be possible to interest a local company in the use of language teaching facilities. Such a laboratory would have to be positioned, designed and equipped to attract commercial users. At the same time the infrastructure would have to support the commercial user in terms of parking, signage, lighting, security and the like.

New opportunities are not restricted to new facilities. Existing facilities can often be converted to provide alternative uses. The question is not so much 'What do you want?' as 'What do you want to achieve?' There are usually many ways of achieving a specific result. The obvious or historical choice may not be the most effective.

Function and flexibility apply equally to the building elements as to the use. Everyone is aware of the different lives of furnishings, building services and components and the disruption that replacement causes. An understanding of the need to maintain, repair and replace building and plumbing elements in the future will lead to design solutions which minimise or eliminate the potential disruption.

Brick and block

In considering the fabric of a building or its external works, a prime consideration must be the external appearance. All projects considered in this article will be the subject of public debate even if they are exempt from planning controls. All providers of capital works also have to consider environmental aspects. This not only refers to the fabric but to the use of energy, water, non-recyclable materials and so on.

A further consideration is the life expectancy of the building or building elements. Buildings may be:

- temporary, a few months – air supported structures such as inflatable buildings;

- short-term, a few years – portable buildings;

- medium-term, 20 years – panel systems;

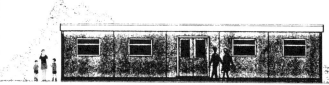

- long-term, 100 years – traditional masonry construction.

Regardless of their original use expectancy, we all realise that temporary often becomes short-term or even medium-term. This is a purely practical factor which must be considered from the outset in construction methods, materials and location.

Brief and budget

What should by now be becoming apparent is the need for a clear plan communicated to all those affected and involved.

At inception, there is often a tendency to rush too soon to a solution rather than explore the alternatives fully. The question should be 'How can we provide more hot meals?' rather than 'How can we get a larger kitchen and dining room?' At inception, the approach should remain flexible to allow the feasbility study to explore all aspects.

The feasibility study should address:

- function – primary, secondary, tertiary;
- timing – feasibility, mobilisation, construction milestones and restraints;
- cost – capital (in use and replacement) cash flow;
- flexibility;
- durability;
- resources – expertise and experience, management, design, execution;
- client functions – users, paymaster, authorisations, neighbours.

Budgets must:

- be realistic;
- contain all elements including contingency;
- be based on thorough programmes;
- fully reflect the brief (ie the result of the feasibility study);
- be fully understood by those affected;

IF YOU'D RATHER CONCENTRATE ON YOUR PUPILS, CAST AN EYE OVER OUR PROPERTY SERVICES.

Professional, cost-effective property management can play a vital part in the success of your school. Firstly, it can help reduce your total running costs. Secondly, it allows you to concentrate on your pupils. Our vast experience of property management means that we can meet any challenge swiftly and efficiently. In fact, you'll find our services are top class. Among the services we offer are:

ESTATE
S U R V E Y I N G

BUILDING SURVEYING
A N D   S P E C I A L I S T
S E R V I C E S

PROJECT
M A N A G E M E N T

DESIGN

FACILITIES
M A N A G E M E N T

MAINTENANCE
S E R V I C E S

For full details,
contact our Head Office:

**ASHBURNER HOUSE,
SEYMOUR GROVE,
OLD TRAFFORD,
MANCHESTER M16 0JL.
TEL: 061-954 6644
FAX: 061-954 6400**

other offices include:

**CARLISLE; PRESTON;
LIVERPOOL; COLWYN BAY;
HAVERFORDWEST; CARDIFF;
BIRMINGHAM; NOTTINGHAM;
LEICESTER.**

234

SIMPLIFYING THE PROPERTY CHALLENGE

Among the challenges posed by the Local Management Reform programme, one of the most complex and cost-sensitive is that of property management.

Against an already difficult background of repair and maintenance issues – and differing divisions of responsibility between schools and their local education authority – schools managers face the need to make rapid progress up the learning curve of 'managing the estate'. This means grasping a whole range of issues, from essential repairs to energy management, from health and safety issues to grounds maintenance.

The sheer breadth of the property challenge, with its 'management time' and budget sensitivities, indicates a key role for external consultancies in guiding both the strategy and progression of changing property regimes.

And for the pressing task of managing within severe resource constraints, educationalists will find plenty of market expertise.

Accelerated by the economic recession recent trends in the building and property industries are much to the advantage of school managers in addressing their total 'estate' needs. The dominant themes have been a growing emphasis on a 'package' approach to construction and building management, and increasingly overlap between the activities and services of the formerly quite distinct property professions.

'Design and Build'; 'Facilities Management' and 'Planned Maintenance' have become key indicators of the trends towards packaged services. Increased competition for recession-hit workloads has also brought sharply increased focus on the customer's needs and competitive value-for-money.

Although the 'multi-discipline' theme has become prominent in the marketing approach of the property industry, comparatively few organisations can boast equal strengths, resources and experience across all the specialisms. Even fewer offer 'in house' capabilities that can truly be deployed and effectively managed over a wide geographical area without sub-contraction.

An exception is PSA Building Management (PSABM), which has an unrivalled range and depth of experience in meeting the varied and often highly complex demands of the public sector.

Its largest business is PSA Building Management Manchester (BMM), covering the whole of North West England, the Midlands and Wales – and among the UK's biggest professional, multi-discipline organisations. Through 10 main offices throughout its region BMM operates as six complementary businesses, able to meet client-determined needs on a consultancy 'menu' or fully integrated 'package' basis.

For example, the *Facilities Management* service offers a comprehensive, planned approach to building and mechanical/electrical maintenance planning, management – building administration and round-the-clock emergency response. These skills are complemented by *Maintenance Services* with a large craft and direct labour force highly experienced in the general building trades and maintenance of utilities.

For both refurbishment and newbuild projects, a multi-disciplinary and CAD-assisted *Design* team covers feasibility; planning/programming; contract advice and strategy; 'fast track' services; heritage specialists and landscape design/environmental conservation.

Design is often partnered by *Project Management*, ensuring progression to client's timescale, cost and quality requirements.

Equally in the 'professional services' stream, BMM's *Building Surveying* service embraces surveys; building law; defect investigation and specialist services including fire protection; health and safety and energy conservation. *Estate* covers property investment appraisal; strategic planning; acquisition; management; disposal and professional services.

Given its deliberate audit and priority-sensitive approach, managers of school estates large or small will find BMM consultancy a logical starting point in simplifying the challenge posed by their increasing responsibilities for property care.

- allocate clear responsibilities;

- reflect available funding.

Budgets which contain unrealistically low expectations of cost will soon run out of cash: much, if not all, the effort will have been wasted; similarly, 'safe' high-budget costs will prevent viable schemes going ahead.

Programme and progress

Similar comments apply to the provision of programmes as to budgets referred to above – both are methods of controlling resources.

Time, however, is in short supply. You might be able to 'buy' time but in any case it is unlikely to be good value for money. It is certain that if you do not plan the proper use of resources and sequencing of events the work will cost more overall.

There is a tendency to programme on-site construction operations in detail but not the elements of design and planning which precede the construction work on the building site. Time lost in the pre-construction stages can have greater impact on works than is often appreciated.

The purpose of plans (programmes or budgets) is twofold: to communicate to those involved the 'what' and 'when' and so on, and to monitor actual achievement against plan. The control aspects are as important as the communication aspects.

Progress monitoring should be simple and fast in order that adverse trends do not go unchecked.

A further aspect is pro-active programme management. This is the ability to monitor trends and, by applying experience, predict adverse trends before they occur and so prevent them. It may sound like 'magic' but it is something most experienced professionals do, often without realising it. Pro-active programme management is using this combination of fact and experience in a planned manner.

Finally, on the subject of time, clearly establish the degree of urgency in the brief, during the feasibility study. Clearly identify the key dates for access, term times and the restraints such as authorisation meetings. Consider different programmes, faster and slower and alternative sequences of doing the work, before you settle on the preferred solution. A time contingency should also be added. In programming terminology this is called 'float'. Just like budgets, programmes have to be realistic.

Specification and serviceability

It is important that the specification and scope of works reflect the real needs of the project. Low or incomplete specification may give a low initial cost but high maintenance costs and short life. If capital is in short supply then the acceptance of short life, basic accommodation or high maintenance costs may need to be considered – provided always that all alternatives are considered on the same basis.

The outline specification is the key to the planned control of quality throughout the design, procurement and construction phases. The final outcome of the specification and quality management is the serviceability of the building.

There is a wide choice of procurement and contract methods available, each of which has its place. Refinements and new methods are continually being introduced. This trend is fairly recent. A few years ago the choice was limited and fairly straightforward.

It requires special expertise to consider these options, assess their implications and make relevant recommendations. The circumstances of the project and the degree of risk the client wishes to allocate to others make each procurement decision unique. Clients should be aware of the wide choice and beware of fashion and advice based on limited experience of the options available.

The role of professional advisers

Professional advice is worthwhile provided it is truly independent, experienced and understanding of the needs of all parties involved. Some advice may be self-serving – the objective being to gain further employment.

The first stage, and possibly the most important, is the feasibility stage. At this stage all options are open and investigation of all the alternative solutions provides the basis of a successful scheme. Assistance at the feasibility stage is very important, particularly the ability to provide novel solutions.

An important point to appreciate at the feasibililty stage is that feasibility studies carried out 'in-house' often come forward with a political response rather than a pragmatic solution. An independent adviser can draw from the client organisation key strategic objectives without undue influence from departmental pressures.

The result of the feasibility stage should be a report clearly setting out all the options and expected outcomes. From the feasibility report the strategy for the project is chosen. This is the foundation of a successful capital project.

Project consultancies are able to provide complete feasibility studies, strategic advice or assistance.

Once the project strategy is determined, project consultants can provide ongoing independent advice to clients during the design, procurement, construction and commissioning stages. This independent role is particularly relevant where the client decides to employ a single-package agreement with no other advisers appointed.

Project consultants are often called upon by clients to give an independent assessment of the current and future state of a project. This 'project audit' is relevant where costs appear to be above budget, delays seem apparent or quality is poor and the client seeks guidance on the facts and his available options to correct the problems.

Choosing professional advisers

Professional advice of the correct type and quality is often difficult to locate, particularly without relevant experience of capital works management. Referrals from colleagues and friends can be a good source, as are directories, promotions, professional institutions and advertisements. There is no single recommended source.

However, having established a long list of project consultants you have to reduce this to a short one – and make an appointment. This could well be an initial short-term appointment to test the choice!

In making your decisions predetermined, objective criteria should be written down. Review promotional literature, request written proposals (in reply to a questionnaire) and conduct interviews.

Your criteria for choosing project consultants should be divided between essential and desirable factors.

- The quality of the individual members of the project consultant team is crucial as is their ability to work together and with the client's staff (personal chemistry and individual confidence are also very important).

- Does the structure and philosophy of the project consultant organisation match and sympathise with the client's organisation?

- What direct and relevant experience do the project consultants have as individuals?

- Do you believe that the project consultants have the ability to perform all the required tasks from a technical, managerial and political view?

Further, there are the desirability factors such as:

- office location;
- fees charged;
- size of organisation;
- familiarity with details.

The desirability factors are only used to choose between project consultants who have satisfied all the essential factors.

Conclusions

- Capital works projects require skill, experience, planning, monitoring and management in order to be successful.

- The early stages of a capital works project are particularly important in determining the likelihood of success.

- Most clients require some professional assistance in managing projects, particularly in determining the strategy.

- During the work stages, clients may require independent advice.

- If clients feel capital projects are not proceeding as planned, they may then commission an independent audit to determine the current state and likely outcome.

- The choice of independent advisers should be objective based on predetermined criteria.

- *Well-managed capital works projects meet their quality and cost objectives and are completed on time.*

BURO FOUR
PROJECT SERVICES

Buro Four Project Services is an independent professional company, comprising thirty staff and offering a full range of project services.

We provide services to property, construction and industry in the locality, to the capital, throughout the country and abroad.

Project Management

Professional Construction Management

Programming, Planning and Co-ordination

Surveying and Contract Services

Assessments of Static Buildings for purchase (and enhancement)

Appraisals of "Live Projects"

BURO FOUR
PROJECT SERVICES

296-300 St John Street, London EC1V 4PP
Telephone: 071-833 8663, Fax: 071-833 8560

241

Part Seven

New Technology

KOGAN PAGE

Educational Management Series

For details
of other
Kogan Page
educational
books call:
071 278 0433

Teacher Training in Secondary Schools
Rowie Shaw

As their responsibilities for teacher training grow, schools are having to scrutinise their role as training providers. Complete with sample materials, this book offers practical advice on many training matters relating to teacher development.

£14.95 Paperback **Order no: KR637** April 1992

Generating Income for Educational Institutions
John Wheale

Practical guidance on how to prepare a business plan to generate income using an institution's own resources, such as training and consultancy, is given by the author of this informative book.

£14.95 Paperback **Order no: KR404** 1991

Marketing for Schools
David Pardey

Marketing principles and how they can best be used to promote a school's services are explained clearly in this logical book. Topics covered include: strategic management, understanding the market, defining your product and developing a promotional strategy for schools.

£14.95 Paperback **Order no: KR464** 1991

Management in Education
A Professional Approach
Vivian Williams

Instead of the usual top–down approach to management, the author of this book emphasises team building as the key to a positive working atmosphere and effective school. A 3–5 year model for staff and school development is included.

£14.95 Paperback **Order no: KR554** June 1992

*Kogan Page books are available from booksellers or from the publisher. To order call **Kogan Page Customer Services** on **071 278 0433** or write to:*

Kogan Page, 120 Pentonville Rd, London N1 9JN

Information Technology in School Management

Alan J Wilcox

The topic of Information Technology (IT) in school management is one which arouses a range of responses varying from extreme apathy to hostility among managers. For many school managers who have no background in IT, the introduction of computers into school offices as a spin-off from Local Management of Schools (LMS) is more likely to be seen as adding problems, rather than assisting with their solutions. Before suggesting ways in which a more positive approach may be developed, it is important that the reasons for the present situation are understood.

The background

In LEAs where steps were taken, before LMS schemes were implemented, to introduce computers into school management as part of the Authority's information management policy, a considered approach to implementation and to training might have been possible. In recent years however, the pressure for change has been such that many Authorities have not had the time, or the resources, to prepare schools adequately. This lack of resources is not merely financial. There are few sources of advice and sound practice on IT in school management precisely because of the speed of the changes that have affected both the educational world and that of IT over the past few years.

Computers have, in fact, been used as an aid to school administration for at least 15 years, though at the outset the computer would not have been in the school. The earliest timetabling projects needed facilities that could only be provided by large companies, university departments, or LEAs, and it was only after the introduction of the personal computer that schools could aspire to having computers on site. These were of limited use for administrative purposes at first, as it required a degree of technical expertise to use them that the vast majority of school managers and office staff did not possess. As a result, computers were often introduced into schools by enthusiasts, and used for curriculum (and recreational) purposes by staff and pupils, but they were often isolated from the school management by the comprehension (and generation) gap. Government initiatives to encourage computing in the curriculum only gradually reduced this gap, most notably through the increased use of word-processing, and the fact that even low-powered machines gave increasing numbers of staff an interest in and experience of computing, which they carried with them into posts of responsibility. Many departments were using BBC and Nimbus computers, for example, to produce set lists and prepare worksheets long before the school office (or the Education Office) had bought its first word-processor.

The past five years have seen an accelerating rate of change, not only as a result of government legislation on education, but in the technology available to assist in school management as distinct from administration. The power of the personal computer has increased at a rate unforeseen by most people ten years ago, and its cost in real terms has fallen equally dramatically. The increased power has brought greater flexibility of use, the ability to store and process vast amounts of information, and the real possibility of using the computer as a management aid, rather than as a replacement for the typewriter.

The need for training

Many managers in schools still treat the computer with suspicion and mistrust, and are reluctant to recognise its potential value. When it arrives as an adjunct to LMS it may be seen as imposing

training requirements and an investment of time that has to compete with all the other urgent demands that local management makes on office staff and management teams. In addition, the 'we managed quite well without it' syndrome is widespread and well established in many schools, and although this can be dismissed as merely a defensive reaction, it is a real problem when it hinders the effective use of management information in a school.

To some extent the responsibility for fostering a positive approach to IT in school management must lie with the LEA. A training programme which concentrates exclusively on the technicalities of the computer and its programes, without taking account of the management implications of introducing the new technology, will not meet the needs of the schools. Management training in preparation for LMS which is too narrowly focused on the detailed financial aspects of the impending changes, may leave schools unprepared for the curricular and organisational developments which will be forced on them by recent legislation. If the LEA does not offer appropriate training for all its schools, the initiative must be taken by the schools themselves, either by putting pressure on the LEA to do so, or by taking advice from sources outside the LEA. Areas where school managers are likely to need training include:

- management of time, in relation to the IT equipment, ie who will use it, when and for what purposes;

- planning the computerisation of administration, ie setting targets and a timescale;

- the computer as a management aid, ie its role in analysis, reporting and planning/budget modelling.

Evaluating IT's contribution

A thorough evaluation of the contribution that IT can make to the management of the school is essential, and will need to take into account not only immediate needs, but also the impending demands which the recording and reporting of National Curriculum assessments, attendance and examination results will make on the teaching and support staff.

This may be self-evaluation, it may be an evaluation by LEA staff working with the school, or it may be an evaluation by a consultant. (Consultancy does not necessarily imply employing an 'expert', who may well charge a large fee for employing his/her management expertise, but could more usefully involve informal discussion with colleagues from other schools or LEAs who are known to have developed 'good practice' in this area.) In addition, assistance might be sought from the Secondary Heads' Association (SHA) and National Association of Head Teachers (NAHT) which are both working on ways of providing a consultancy service for their members in various areas of school management.

A management information policy

The school management team must accept the responsibility for establishing and implementing a management information policy. This is essential if necessary information is to be collected, stored and used effectively, at a time when schools are being asked for more information to be made available more widely. A further consideration is the legal framework within which schools must operate. This embraces not only data security, but also copyright (on software), and all staff need to be aware of their responsibilities in this area.

Whether or not the headteacher takes the leading role in implementing such a policy, for it to be successful he or she must show commitment to it, and give active support to whoever is taking the lead, since management of change and human resource management will be major aspects of the task.

The equipment

So far little emphasis has been placed on the actual technology, on the software which schools will use to manage their ever-increasing store of information. To give brief guidelines on computing equipment is a thankless task, as almost any advice is likely to be out-of-date by publication date, and not all experts will agree on what is the best solution to a school's IT needs.

Most schools will have been supplied with IT equipment on the basis of an assessment of their needs by the LEA IT Services Department, modified by the available financial resources. Although there may be questions as to the adequacy of funding, and the appropriateness of the equipment and software provided, in the end schools have two alternatives, (after formulating their management information policy and assessing their needs): either to make the best use of what is provided, or make the extension of their system a management priority, using devolved or private funds.

If the latter option is chosen, care must be taken to work closely with the LEA. Schools need to be certain that equipment is reliable, compatible with that provided by the LEA, and preferably covered by the LEA's support and maintenance services. Going it alone may have its attractions (in the form of an apparently cheaper solution, or one that is not influenced by a centralist policy on IT) but can cause problems in the long run, as few schools can afford the specialist services that the LEA can share in, as part of the County or Borough Council. It is important that school managers obtain good advice, based on specialist knowledge, when considering additions to their school computer systems. Often this will be found in their Local Authority IT Services Department and the LEA LMS support teams, especially in relation to the price, quality and reliability of equipment. The application of IT to school management is a specialist area in its own right, requiring as much, if not more, knowledge of schools as of computing, and it is for this reason that emphasis was placed on a thorough evaluation of the school's management needs in the light of LMS and IT, if necessary with external assistance, earlier in this chapter.

Similar criteria apply to the software. Most schools will receive an LEA-approved package which normally includes word-processing, database, and financial management modules. They may also receive curriculum management programs, particularly if the LEA is using a system such as SIMS, and sometimes spreadsheet facilities. In addition, most LEAs provide communications software to enable data and other material to be transmitted electronically between the schools and the administrative centre. If schools are dissatisfied with the LEA package, before deciding to add to it, or adopt any alternative, they must take into account all the factors relating to the transfer of data between schools, and between school and LEA, and also the question of software support and training. Here too, going it alone could prove to be a hazardous exercise, in that it might involve the school in additional work to produce financial and other information for the LEA, and expensive if all training and support has to be paid for.

CHECKLIST

- Does your LEA have a policy or code of practice on data security standards?

- Does your school have a management information policy which includes the above, and which provides guidance for staff on the collection, storage and use of data?

- Has the management team made a careful assessment of the priorities in using IT for administration, having regard to the organisational changes, and changes in working practices that LMS, and an increased use of IT, will involve?

- Has the school identified its training needs:

    - for senior staff who need to appreciate the potential of IT as a whole school management aid?

    - for middle managers who could use IT to increase efficiency in their areas of responsibility?

    - for support staff who are often called upon to use IT to carry out a task, the complexity of which is only dimly perceived by the manager, who knows 'that you get that from the computer'?

Making best use of IT for management

In conclusion, it is important that neither the difficulties nor the rewards of implementing a policy of extending the use of IT in school management are underestimated. To build up and maintain a pupil data-base takes time and care. To learn to use it effectively will also take time and training. The same is true of the effective use of personnel and financial data. However, a school must be prepared to invest time and effort in setting up its management information system, if it is to make the best use of its resources as a whole. Teachers (and especially senior managers) are resources which are too expensive to be wasted on routine clerical and administrative tasks. These can be done more efficiently by support and clerical staff, who will often see in IT opportunities for greater job satisfaction and improved career prospects, particularly if the school is able to offer higher salaries to those who are prepared to acquire a higher level of skills.

LMS is intended to enable schools to use resources more effectively in order to enhance pupil learning, and IT has a major part to play in achieving this objective. By helping them to meet the increasing administrative pressures which LMS and other recent innovations have imposed on them, IT can assist schools to focus their resources (and in particular their teaching resources) more closely on the curricular and developmental needs of the pupils.

Further reading

1 Bird, Patrick, *Microcomputers in School Administration*, Hutchinson Education, now Stanley Thornes, 1984 and 1986
2 FAST (Federation Against Software Theft) 2, Lake End Court, Taplow, Maidenhead, Berkshire S16 0JQ   Tel. 0628 660377. For a model policy on the use of computer software within an organisation.
3 Wilcox, Alan, *Managing with Information Technology*, SHA, 1992.

254

Computer Networking Systems Within the School

Brian Kennedy

When asked the question 'Why do we put computers in schools?', answers range from the erudite 'in order to help reflect the outside world' to the more cynical 'because the government wanted them there'. These somewhat constrained views of the use of the hardware/software elements of information technology (IT) are at once both disappointing and ill-conceived.

The use of IT continues to be a great motivator, but to what avail? There seems little point in motivating the child or teacher, only to be unable to respond to statements like 'I can never get to use the computers: they're always booked/locked away/broken' – surely a damning indictment on some schools' approaches to such a valuable resource.

Networks

The first attempt to break the 'computer room' syndrome was perversely by continuing to support their existence while encouraging teachers to engage in a booking system. Partially successful only! The single computer in the classroom was tried and found to be of limited use only, and difficult to manage within the context of a lesson. The solution for my own LEA was to install networks.

Most schools in this LEA now have a minimum network system

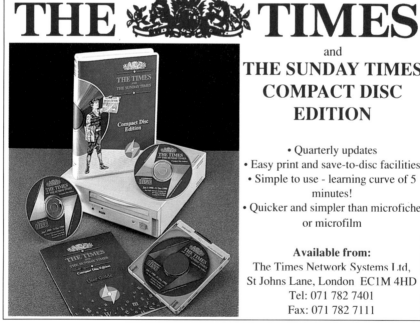

in excess of a kilometre with 60 plus computers, while some are over three kilometres and support more than 100 computers. This philosophy of large-scale network systems has undoubtedly removed a great deal of the burden of management from the end users. No more need to expend mountains of chalk, pins, dust and the like on filling up those holes in floppy discs.

Using networks effectively

What are the criteria by which one might judge the effective use or otherwise of installing large networks? The following three may be useful.

1. *Management of resources*

There is very clearly a human management function to any computer hardware. The effective management and support of stand-alone systems requires much time to be expended in keeping discs catalogued, 'clean' and functioning in spite of the school environment! Is this a job for a professional teacher?

Local hard discs provide little amelioration to the problem since, because of their open and accessible environments, they may act as a catalyst and a challenge to some pupils to engage in wiping them clean. It is all very well having hard-disc capability but at what human cost? How much time will a computer manager need to spend reformatting individual discs? Is this time productive?

2. *Sharing resources*

At the simplest level, networks allow the cost-effective sharing of resources such as printers, hard discs, CD ROM and the like. Although there is a simple financial equation to govern cost saving here, there is also a human cost. An on-site network manager *is* required but this is now a teacher who also undertakes the duties of IT curriculum coordinator. Thus her/his time could be largely devoted to encouraging the use of IT in supporting curriculum development rather than being overburdened by technical issues.

This has very fundamental implications on how a school offers a sufficiently wide range of IT experiences to children. Too much time spent supporting a fragile software/hardware interface may mean insufficient time available for real IT coordination.

3. Standard systems

There are undoubted gains in both curricular and technical terms of having standard systems installed. Standard hardware running a range of software under a standard front end is supported by my own LEA. A small support team of advisory teachers is thus able to support this model very effectively since the system 'appears' similar in each school. As a coincidence, this model strongly encourages self-help groups.

Case study: Dudley LEA

Schools in Dudley LEA have a long history of sharing and mutual support. Trialling new systems in pilot schools is always on the basis of possible future replication in others. The good working relationship between schools and the IT advisory team means that this philosophy works in practice, to the benefit of all Authority schools.

Background

Dudley LEA has been using network systems in secondary schools since they were first introduced. With a strong central support team, some of the technical mystique of networks in schools was dispelled. This has allowed time for school coordinators to concentrate on curriculum development using the technology. The benefits are not difficult to see: all schools have produced an IT action plan, as part of their school development plan, enabling IT to become an integral part of (and an enhancement to) the learning process. Straightforward access to generic and subject specific software is via an LEA written front end.

The pattern of deployment was traditionally one or two computer rooms together with a number of single-site stations. However, it is in the nature of this style of deployment to enhance the closed learning environment further.

Fortuitously, more powerful 32-bit technology became available and made the consideration of the educational uses of more powerful tools a necessity. The problem was the dilemma of whether to support this more powerful technology in stand-alone form – with all the associated management and disc problems – or to connect them to networks. The first is not a viable choice: we are working with real teachers here who have little time spare to organise their lessons, much less get involved in organising banks of stand-alone machines. The second is possible, but since teachers have been led to believe that we have moved on since the days of cassette tape loading speeds, was not seriously considered.

The resolution of this problem must also aid the change to a more open-access learning environment and build on what has gone before, both in terms of hardware and expertise. Thus a fundamental change in hardware was ruled out.

The solution: fast-star networks

It was decided to install fast-star networks utilising disc sharers and to help schools move towards deploying their computers in open-access clusters. In truth, two schools had already started to do this, so there is real evidence of the difficulties and successes of this manoeuvre.

This new deployment pattern means small clusters of computers, typically five to eight, attached to a disc sharer and to the local area network. Network traffic is organised and divided to allow most work to be internal to the cluster with messaging and so on to use the main network backbone. Such clusters must have a minimum configuration of generic software and a high-quality printer. In this way, more powerful computers share the hard-disc sharer and thus have high-speed access to applications. Additionally, they are connected to local area network for communications with eight-bit technology in other parts of the campus.

Users, at log on, are connected to the applications on the disc sharer *and* to their own personal directories on local area network. Users continue to operate on local area network as before, but can communicate with the more powerful technology. In this way a good degree of future proofing is built in to purchases. The message must be that the 'old' technology still has much useful life and can co-exist with the more powerful systems in an educational environment.

In such a way children can be encouraged to choose the most suitable tool for the work.

Lessons and conclusions

Any such change in topology will only be successful where there is a clear intention by *all* users to see computer hardware as a truly shared resource. There is no point in changing deployment pattern simply in order to share computers 'geographically around the school'. The confusion between computers across the curriculum and computers in every classroom is a model to be avoided!

It is essential that the child should have reasonable access to hardware without the need to book 'three weeks in advance'. Unless the hardware is deployed in such a fashion as to positively encourage open access then pupils, and more especially staff, will always view the new technology resource as something rather special and not for them.

A more open access to new technology can help engender a critical approach to a variety of learning techniques. All doing the same thing at the same time is not always the most appropriate method. The teacher as facilitator and the child as a contracted partner in the learning process has long been seen as desirable but rarely achievable in practice. Open access to IT resources can help.

Change is in the nature of IT resources: we are becoming used to seeing the latest pieces of software and hardware try to outdo their rivals. Some of the changes have been positive and beneficial, and we need to build on these and identify how best we can provide our children with the opportunities for actually using IT systems as part of their entitlement curriculum.

The development of the use of computers in the secondary phase owes a great deal to the concurrent development of the use of networks. Such networks in their raw state, although physically operational, require very considerable development work to make them more user-friendly and reliable.

In this case, the development work has been carried out by the Dudley LEA IT team and groups of teachers in our schools. Countless person hours have been invested in developing and tailoring these systems to our use and as a consequence all secondary schools have enjoyed the support of a standard system. A small number of primary schools have also had these network systems installed.

Standardisation of the system was fundamental to the quality of ongoing support available and has been one of the major influences in the development of educational computing in Dudley secondary establishments. Much of the technical nature of the network system is hidden from student and staff users, who approach the software and hardware as IT users, rather than IT experts. In

addition, the network system itself is used as an exemplar teaching tool in computer studies and IT courses at key stages 3 and 4.

Such has been the success of network systems that IT co-ordinators have been able to concentrate on the educational uses of IT within the educational context, relatively free from the constraints imposed by lack of technical expertise. In cases where co-ordinators have expressed a technical interest, INSET has been provided to extend and develop this important aspect. It is one of the features of the development of the educational use of IT in Dudley that progress is invariably through the sharing of technical knowledge.

Management of such systems is the responsibility of school-based IT co-ordinators working in partnership with advisory teachers at the educational computer centre. Typically, school-based managers have some allocated free time for this task, although the quantity varies from school to school. In all cases, systems are connected to the central system, via modem and telephone line, and a coherent and comprehensive network of hardware, software and support has grown up in the Dudley LEA.

Thus the philosophy and practice of supporting networked computers has been used to considerable benefit, for all children in the secondary phase.

Summary

Although hard-disc-based stand-alone machines may provide a solution, they in turn generate a new series of problems: unrestricted access to hard discs, management and control of contents, the use of floppy discs for personal storage, back up of hard discs and no shared peripheral devices are but a few.

The proof is evident: network systems of computers in this LEA have been developed for students and teachers alike, and their use is a testament to their success. The maxim, 'It's used because it works and it works because it's used' is still most appropriate.

Electronic Registration System

Grant Milne

Introduction

For many years now, institutions such as schools and colleges have been dependent upon an age-old system of using a manual register to keep records of pupils and their attendance. As educational needs have changed with split-site schools, colleges with remote annexes it would seem appropriate to review the system which monitors the attendance and movements of pupils.

In line with new government policy, it will soon be compulsory for each school to make public its attendance figures. This will reflect on schools' ability to maintain pupils' interests in subjects and also on methods of keeping truancy in check.

Through correct use of this information, it is possible to foresee where attendance problems can begin, and efforts can be made to correct these before they escalate to uncontrollable levels. Attendance figures themselves can also be used in the management of a school or college for identifying empty classrooms, class numbers and time spent on various subjects; by the use of historical data drawn from these figures, a better understanding of future requirements can be gained.

We can see that accurate and reliable registration information is a key to reducing truancy, and can be used to assist in the efficient management of a school or college.

The existing method

Registration

The existing method of registration, in use since the beginning of the education system, had only one initial purpose: to keep a record of pupil attendance.

Since then, education bodies have tried to obtain more information from it: by collating the data in whatever form they chose it has been possible to obtain average figures and use this information to help manage the future of the school.

Basic uses

The basic task of registers is very limited. The first use is as a list of pupil attendance in a building or room – of great importance as a checklist for evacuation should a fire or other incident occur. Second is as a record of checking a pupil's attendance. Finally, because details of lateness, sickness or truancy are also stored as coded entries in each square, the register can be used for retrieval of historical data to give a class or pupil's attendance profile.

Expansion

Using the register to extract other information usually entails gathering information from several registers to obtain figures for year, class, subject or pupil attendance.

To assist in this method of collating the data, many bodies now use a microcomputer as a means of storing and manipulating the data into a helpful format.

As schools and colleges find themselves with too little money for resources, uneconomical subjects, shortages of teaching staff or even shortages of classrooms, this type of historical management data is becoming more and more important in the decision-making and future planning of an educational environment.

So where are the problems and how can they be resolved?

Problems

Every system has its faults. The standard register was more than adequate for the information it was originally designed to cope with and with the environment around it to make it work. As pupil numbers increase and the number of schools and colleges decreases, large numbers of pupils have to fill the limited educational space available.

Large numbers of pupils mean large numbers of names on the register. As an example, let's imagine a school with perhaps 1000 pupils. To register them, a roll must be taken – usually once in the morning and once in the afternoon, an administration job of some 15 minutes twice a day.

To make use of the data from the book the school must now enter the data into the computer. One thousand pupils twice a day make 2000 entries a day, five days a week: time-consuming, laborious and repetitive jobs that take a member of the office staff away from doing other tasks and often leads to errors like mistyped information or an absence marked instead of a lateness.

The computer can only work with the data placed within it. To ensure that the pupil attends each lesson, we must take a register each time he or she moves to another workplace. In an extreme case this could be four morning periods and four afternoon periods on

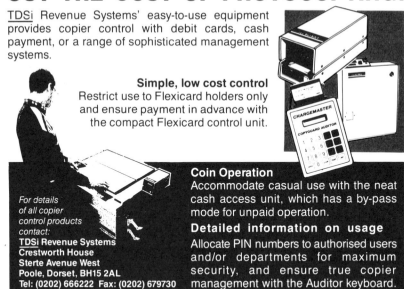

top of a normal registration period. The poor office staff now have a total of 10,000 entries a day to cope with and look forward only to the prospect of another 40,000 for the rest of the week!

The electronic method

Introduction

The use of a bank card to draw money from a 'hole in the wall' has made electronic data collection part of everyday life. The same operation has been applied to record individual attendance. What follows is a brief description of how this operates.

The card

Because we have effectively done away with a register, pupils are issued with 'smart cards' similar to those used in cash machines. A strip of magnetic tape makes the card unique to the individual college or school, and is encoded with two numbers. The first prevents cards from one college working in another. The second makes it unique to each user. The card number is also embossed onto the card itself so that when issuing the card to the pupil or teacher it can be checked.

The card becomes the pupil's enrolment number, making for easier handling of information.

The reader

Having established the first part of the system by using the card to identify the pupil, the second part is to set up a device to take that information and feed it back to the computer. The card 'reader', as it is known, must be set up at points where the old-style register would have been taken: namely, each classroom.

To input the information into the reader all the pupil has to do is run or 'swipe' the card through the reader where a special head reads the information on the magnetic strip and sends it directly back to the central control box and then, in turn, back to the computer.

The computer

Because the information is sent almost instantaneously, we can use the in-built clock on the computer to assign a date and time to the event. The card gives us who, the reader gives us where, and the computer gives us when.

Advantages of electronic registration

- Removes the administration work from the teacher. This gives the registration time back to the school for other subjects.
- Takes away responsibility for all errors in making and submitting the register.
- Feeds the information direct from the classroom to the office.
- Does away with missing registers through loss or theft.
- Sends information instantly the moment 'reading' occurs in the classroom.

LATECOMERS
MISS
THE GOLD FEVER

Add a little gold coloured chip and your vending machine will become a gold-mine. NRI presents a new payment system, consisting of a changer, bill validator and chip card reader. Combined with the GLOBO card, a chip card, it gives a new impetus to the vending machine market.

Purchasing at a vending machine becomes more attractive with the new NRI payment system. The customer can now decide upon the method of payment. As before, he can pay by cash, or he can use the GLOBO card. By using the GLOBO card the customer can purchase whatever he desires from your vending machine.

The GLOBO card can be reloaded by coins or bills whenever the customer wants to.

Due to its modular construction, all vending machines having a mains supply, can be fitted simply and quickly with the new NRI payment system.

For further information please contact us.

National Rejectors, Inc. · Unit 7 · The Pavilion Amber Close · Amington Industrial Estate · Tamworth B77 4RP · Telephone (0827) 62696 · Fax (0827) 62389

systematisch gut.

M5A 178.254en/8.91m

- Inputs the data directly into the computer. Abolishes monotonous keying-in of data. Makes the total data transfer 100 per cent accurate. Gives back staff time to do other office duties.

- Does away with storage needs of registers.

- Gives more accurate management information.

- Gives increased frequency of information. More frequent registers can be taken at little extra cost in time or administration.

- Prevents pupils from absenting themselves after registration.

- Automatic self-check of the data for errors.

- Keeps timetables up to date.

- Allows for automatic reporting of truant pupils, for day or class.

- Makes for fast comparisons of data, and reports on 'unusual' occurrences.

- Expandable to provide registration data at one or many points.

- Allows teachers to check on pupil attendances quickly.

- Registration data available at points of emergency such as fire.

- Expandable to encompass other educational needs. Information available for library system. Information available for access control to restricted rooms and areas. Expandable as identification system for credit type use, such as canteen.

Other applications of smart cards

The vending industry

The proliferation of these magnetic cards has spread to the vending machine industry. Advantages to such 'cashless payment' include:

- the possibility of targeted discounts and subsidies for certain users, such as employees;

STAFF NOTICE BOARD

MEMORANDUM

To: All staff

From: Headmaster

Re: School Pantomime

... decided by the board of ...at this years pantomime
...ER PAN.

...ourt of the Drama Club has
volunteered her services to
the event.

...ff wishing to donate their time
...s worthy cause should please put
...name below.

...k you.

FOR SALE.
£1,100 oNo

- a reduction in vandalism and theft since the machines hold little or no cash;

- a possible increase in use due to greater convenience.

Balancing these plus-points is the fact that, if the machine is solely card-operated, a large number of potential users may be excluded. Thus many machines now accept both card and cash payment.

Recent developments have also included cards that can be used across a range of machines irrespective of manufacturer.

Part Eight

Europe

8.1

European Links

Pat Collings

Allez l'Europe! In 1972 we were asked to decide whether we wanted to enter the Common Market and 'become a part of Europe'. By the end of 1992 the single market will be in place.

Raising awareness

Of the European Community's population of 340 million, 130 million are under the age of 25. The European Parliament has a committee for Youth Affairs, Culture, Education, Information and Sport; numerous directives and resolutions of the European Council relate to the preparation of young people for the transition from education to working life but it is said that the general level of awareness about the European Dimension and the opportunities available in the 1990s is lower among young people in the UK than elsewhere in the Community.

Geographically, the UK has always been part of Europe, and some British people regarded themselves as Europeans long before 1992. Too many people (and too many newspapers), however, speak and write as if we are not really part of Europe. It is the job of schools to recognise the reality of our Europeanness and to educate a generation which must consider itself truly European. Industry and commerce are increasingly aware of the opportunities which the single European market will bring and the urgency of the need to prepare for its advent; Chambers of Commerce have appointed

European Advisers and provide intensive language courses for their members. In schools there are many strategies which can be adopted to realise the objective of preparing our young people to be European citizens.

Modern foreign language teaching

A modern foreign language is included in the National Curriculum as a foundation subject with the requirement that at least one language should be studied during key stages 3 and 4. Schools must offer at least one of the eight working languages of the European Community.

The 'Initial Advice' stresses that learning a language encourages respect for the attitudes and customs of other countries and of the communities making up the society in the area in which children live. In particular the working group points out that 'for Britain as a trading nation competence in foreign languages will be of crucial importance in a rapidly changing and increasingly competitive world. The creation of the Single European Market is but one pointer to those changing circumstances. Our pupils will need to be prepared for a world where greater skills in modern foreign languages will be much in demand. We need to be able to talk to our trading partners in their own languages'. Securing language provision is thus a *sine qua non*, marrying the acquisition of linguistic skill with the development of positive attitudes to other cultures. Schools are urged to diversify so that a language other than French is no longer seen as the preserve of a talented few but is available to a reasonable number of pupils of all abilities.

Using communications technology

In delivering the National Curriculum for modern languages, the expansion of the use of audio, video and Information Technology will open up new opportunities for communicative activities such as the exchange of electronic mail between British and other European schools. At key stage 4 of the National Curriculum, for example, students should be able to telex a message in the modern language studied. Digitised video-tape might be used for a report on an exchange visit. Medium-term planning for acquiring the appropriate communications technology for all of this needs to be included in the school development plan.

Using foreign language assistants

Foreign language assistants have long been recognised by modern languages teachers as vital motivators; living proof that the language is used by real people with first-hand experience of families, schools, towns and villages where the language is actually used as a means of communication! Local Management enables schools to decide how many assistants to engage; current evidence suggests that heads and governors recognise how cost effective the language assistants are as demand is steadily rising across the country. In terms of European awareness the assistant can be effectively deployed not only in the languages department but, for example, in Geography, History or Business Studies or as a visitor in a structured interview for Personal and Social Education. Children in partner primary schools in the area can meet the assistant as a taste of exciting learning ahead.

Exchange visits

It is through contact with native speakers (the assistant and others) that an appreciation of the similarities and differences between cultures within the Community can be addressed. Links with schools abroad can be the source of valuable authentic materials such as audio and video recordings, magazines and newspapers, objects and photographs. Ideally of course as many children as possible should experience an exchange visit to the home of a child in the exchange school. No other single experience has such potential for both cultural and linguistic learning but few schools are able to make this happen for all their students. Nevertheless all children can benefit from a school exchange by arranging for the European visitors to be hosted for a day by children who cannot take a full part in an exchange or by arranging structured joint activities in the languages classroom. Corresponding with children in the exchange school can give a unique relevance to, say, a survey of the relative popularity of sport in European countries or an investigation into co-operative European ventures such as pollution control.

Exchanges for teachers

Serving teachers can diversify or improve their language skills by exchanges or short language courses or gain experience of educational practices in other countries of the EC through several programmes administered by the Central Bureau for Exchanges and Visits, which is the UK national office responsible for the provision of information and advice on all forms of educational visits and exchanges. Exchanges can be as short as three weeks for a post-to-post job swap, or for longer periods of a term or a year in Austria, Belgium, Denmark, France, Germany, Italy and Spain. The exchange teacher's travel costs can be covered in full as well as funding for a preliminary visit if the exchange is for longer than a term. Short courses for teachers of modern languages supported by bursaries are also organised by The Central Bureau in Germany, France, Spain and Italy. Study visits to set up work experience in France or Spain, for example, can also attract financial support from the in-service training department of the Central Bureau.

Cross-curricular projects

The European dimension is a cross-curricular theme of the National

Curriculum for which NCC guidance will be issued; many of the attainment targets concerned with environmental issues in Science, for example, could easily be studied in a European context. Information on teaching about Europe can be found in *Euroednews* and the *European Dimension in Teaching* (*EDIT*) a journal obtainable from the UK Centre for European Education (UKCEE). A number of Databases can be interrogated in French or German (eg Campus 2000), schools can be linked by computer to the French Minitel system; these facilities could be useful for many curriculum areas. Joint curriculum projects may attract sponsorship under the Central Bureau's European Awareness programme while entering for the annual European schools and colleges competition can produce the necessary stimulus for imaginative responses to topics such as Tourism or the Environment. Again details are available from the UKCEE.

Eighteen LEAs are participating in European Awareness development projects. These range from European history field studies to the production of a multi-national, multi-lingual newspaper, shared outdoor education activity or a European awareness programme for children with learning difficulties. A report of experiences from the pilot project is already available from the Central Bureau; the report provides ideas for action at school, college and LEA levels.

Opportunities for women

Article 119 enshrines gender issues in the Treaty of Rome and is the subject of the third Action Plan. By the turn of the century 50 per cent of the workforce will be women; already 40 per cent of new companies are started by women. The single market will bring more opportunities for women; the challenge is the quality of the jobs available to them. Schools need to address their equal opportunities policies and practices in order to prepare women for their role in Europe. Professor Charles Handy puts it starkly: 'Countries which recognise the worth of female brains are going to get more of the talent. Britain must wake up to the fact that a lot of the most exciting and interesting talent comes from young women, or we're going to lose them to Europe.'

Work experience in Europe

Careers teams in school might consider extending a work experience programme to include a European option. The European Work Experience Project can help to find placements in business, manufacture, commerce or services. With good preparation of students and companies work experience in Europe motivates further learning before, during and after the week itself. It brings co-operative learning for staff and students not only in linguistic skills but in understanding the similarities and differences in the workplace.

Motivating your school

Positive attitudes from the staff in all departments is a key to success in taking the school into Europe. These can be fostered via a special event such as a simulation exercise organised by students for parents, governors and the local community, complete with atmospheric music, visual aids and food!

Finally, active encouragement can be given to support participation in shared activity holidays for young people from two or more European countries or for students at 18 plus to spend some time as a junior language assistant.

QUESTIONS TO ASK

- Is language learning given a high profile by teachers within and outside the languages department?

- Do the languages taught (both European and Community) enjoy equal status?

- Has full consideration been given to the appointment of foreign language assistants?

- Are foreign language assistants deployed effectively?

- Are modern language teachers encouraged to refresh their language skills and/or consider a teacher exchange?

- Has European work experience been considered?

- Have all curriculum areas addressed the European dimension in their schemes of work?

Useful addresses

For further information, see list of useful names and addresses in Part Nine.

Part Nine

Useful Names and Addresses

Useful Names and Addresses

Advisory Conciliation and Arbitration Service (ACAS), 11–12 St. James' Square, London SW1Y 4LA   Tel: 071 210 3600

The Association of British Insurers, Aldermary House, 10/15, Queen Street, London, EC4N 1TT   Tel: 071 248 4477

Association for Language Learning, 16 Regent Place, Rugby CV23 2PN   Tel: 0788 546443

British Comparative and International Education Society, Department of Education, University of Cambridge, 17 Trumpington Street, Cambridge CB2 1QA   Tel: 0223 336294

British Educational Equipment Association, 20 Beausort Court, Admiral's Way, London E14 9XL   Tel: 071 537 4997

Business Schools of Polytechnics/Universities (Check university/polytechnic prospectuses for addresses and contacts)

Business & Technology Education Council, Central House, Upper Woburn Place, London WC1H 0HH   Tel: 071 388 3288

Central Bureau for Educational Visits and Exchanges, Seymour Mews House, Seymour Mews, London W1H 9PE   Tel: 071 486 5101

Centre for Information on Language Teaching and Research, Regent's College, Inner Circle, Regent's Park, London NW1 4NS   Tel: 071 486 8221

The Centre for the Study of Comprehensive Schools, The Queen's Building, University of Leicester, Barrack Road, Northampton NN2 6AF

Chartered Institute of Public Finance and Accountancy (CIPFA), 3 Robert Street, London WC2N 6BH   Tel: 071 930 3456

Chartered Insurance Institute, 20, Aldermanbury, London, EC2C 7HY   Tel: 071 606 3835

City & Guilds of London Institute, 46 Britannia Street, London WC1X 9RG   Tel: 071 278 2468

Commission of the European Communities, 8 Storey's Gate, London SW1P 3AT   Tel: 071 222 8122

Commission for Racial Equality, Elliot House, 10–12 Allington Street, London SW1E 5EH   Tel: 071 828 7022

Communication in Education, 7 Mercia Village, Torwood Close, Westwood Business Park, Coventry CV4 8HX

Council of Local Education Authorities (CLEA), Eaton House, 66 Eaton Square, London SW1 9BH   Tel: 071 235 1200

DES Pensions Branch, Mowden Hall, Staindrop Road, Darlington, DL3 9BG   Tel: 0325 460155

DES Publications' Despatch Centre, Honeypot Lane, Canons Park, Stanmore, Middlesex HA7 1AZ

'Education Matters' Radio 5 programme on educational issues. Contact: Wendy Jones, 'Education Matters', Broadcasting House, Portland Place, London 1A 1AA   Tel: 071 580 4468

Equal Opportunities Commission, Overseas House, Quay Street, Manchester M3 3HN   Tel: 061 883 9244

European Association of Teachers, 20 Brookfield, Highgate West Hill, London N6 6AS   Tel: 081 340 9136

European Cultural Foundation, County End, Bushey Heath WD2 1NY   Tel: 081 950 1057

European Movement, Europe House, 1 Whitehall Place, London SW1A 2HA   Tel: 071 839 6622

European Parliament Information Office, 2 Queen Anne's Gate, London SW1A 9AA   Tel: 071 222 0411

EWE Project, ORT Resource Centre, QM & Westfield Colleges, Kidderpore Avenue, London NW3 7ST   Tel: 071 794 0027

Health Education Authority, Hamilton House, Mabledon Place, London WC1H 9TX   Tel: 071 383 3833

Health and Safety Commission, Regina House, 259 Marylebone Road, London NW1 5RR   Tel: 071 723 1262

Health and Safety Executive (HSE), St Hugh's House, Stanley Precinct, Bootle L20 3QY   Tel: 051 951 4000

Industrial Society, 3 Carlton House Terrace, London SW1 5DG   Tel: 071 839 4300

Local Authorities' Conditions of Service Advisory Board (LACSAB), 41 Belgrave Square, London SW1X 8NZ   Tel: 071 235 6081

Local Government International Bureau, 35 Great Smith Street, London SW1P 3BJ   Tel: 071 222 1636

National Association of Governors and Managers (NAGM), 81 Rustlings Road, Sheffield S11 7AB   Tel: 0742 662467

National and Local Government Officers' Association (NALGO), NALGO House, 1 Mabledon Place, London WC1H 9AJ   Tel: 071 388 2366

National Confederation of Parent/Teacher Associations (NCPTA), 2 Ebbsfleet Industrial Estate, Stonebridge Road, Gravesend, Kent

DA11 9DU   Tel: 0474 560618

National Council for Educational Technology (NCET), 3 Devonshire Street, London W1N 2BA   Tel: 071 580 7553

National Council for Vocational Qualifications, 222 Euston Road, London NW1 2BZ   Tel: 071 387 9898

National Curriculum Council, Albion Wharf, 25 Skeldergate, York YO1 2XL   Tel: 0904 622533

National Union of Public Employees (NUPE), Civic House, 20 Grand Depot Road, Woolwich, London SE18 6SF   Tel: 081 854 2244

Schools Examination and Assessment Council, Newcombe House, 45 Notting Hill Gate, London W11 3JB   Tel: 071 229 1234

Society of Education Officers (SEO), 21–27 Lambs Conduit Street, London WC1N 3NJ   Tel: 071 8831 1973

University Association for Contemporary European Studies, King's College London, Strand, London WC2R 2LS   Tel: 071 240 0206

UK Centre for European Education, Seymour Mews House, Seymour Mews, London W1H 9PE   Tel: 071 486 5101

UK Lingua Unit, Seymour Mews House, Seymour Mews, London W1H 9PE   Tel: 071 486 5101

Part Ten

Directory of Services and Products

**High quality
school furniture
from Germany.**

The inclinable
school table is
available with
steel frame or
wooden frame
to be combined
with steel or
wooden frame
chairs.

For more than a
century VS has been one
of the leading German
manufacturers of high
quality furniture for
schools, higher education
institutions and libraries.
The school tables illustra-
ted here are the latest top
product resulting from
development work
between VS, pedagogues,
orthopaedic and eye
specialists.

The writing surfaces
of these new tables can
be easily and safely
inclined at either 5°, 10°
or 16° in line with the
DIN-ISO standard recom-
mendations and make an
important contribution to
healthy an fatigue-free
seating in schools.

This new and
innovative product is
available in various
versions such as height,
colour and wood or
steel frame.

For further details
of VS's wide range of
products, please write
to the Export Manager,
VS Vereinigte Spezial-
möbelfabriken GmbH & Co,
P. O. Box 14 02,
D-6972 Tauberbischofsheim,
Germany.

Directory of Services and Products

Accountancy

Accounting Answers Ltd
Premier Centre
Luzborough Lane
Romsey
Hampshire SO51 9AQ
Tel: 0794 830355
Fax: 0794 830779

Coopers and Lybrand Deloitte
Chartered Accountants
PO Box 207
128 Queen Victoria Street
London EC4P 4JX
Tel: 071 583 5000
Fax: 071 248 3623

MacIntyre & Co
Chartered Accountants
28 Ely Place
London EC1N 6RL
Tel: 071 242 0242
Fax: 071 405 4786

Neville Russell
Chartered Accountants
246 Bishopgate
London EC2M 4PB
Tel: 071 377 1000
Fax: 071 377 8931

Accrediting bodies

The National Council for
Vocational Qualifications
222 Euston Road
London NW1 2BZ
Tel: 071 387 9898

Scottish Vocational Education
Council (SCOTVEC)
Hanover House
24 Douglas Street
Glasgow G2 7NQ
Tel: 041 248 7900

Air conditioning and ventilation

Drayton Controls
(Engineering) Ltd
Chantry Close
West Drayton
Middlesex UB7 7SP
Tel: 0895 444012
Fax: 0895 421901

Graffiti Clean Ltd
Unit 5, 124A Woodhill
Hillreach
London SE18 5JH
Tel: 081 855 0008
Fax: 081 855 0330

Landis and Gyr
Building Control (UK) Ltd
2 Dukes Meadow
Millboard Road
Bourne End
Buckinghamshire SL8 5XF
Tel: 0628 850808
Fax: 0628 850797

Architects

MEB Partnership
12 Neal's Yard
Covent Garden
London WC2H 9DP
Tel: 071 831 1162
Fax: 071 240 1323

Art and craft

Berol Ltd
Oldmedow Road
King's Lynn
Norfolk PE30 4JR
Tel: 0553 761221
Fax: 0553 766535

GLS Fairway Ltd
Ferry Lane
Tottenham Hale
London N17 9NQ
Tel: 081 801 3333

Hope Education
Orb Mill
Huddersfield Road
Waterhead
Oldham OL4 2ST
Tel: 061 633 6611
Fax: 061 633 3431

MacCulloch and Wallis & Co Ltd
25–26 Dering Street
London W1R 0BH
Tel: 071 629 0311
Fax: 071 491 2481

Audio visual

GLS Fairway Ltd
Ferry Lane
Tottenham Hale
London N17 9NQ
Tel: 081 801 3333

Don Gresswell Ltd
Bridge House
Grange Park
London N21 1RB
Tel: 081 360 6622
Fax: 081 360 9231

Unicol Engineering
Green Road
Headington
Oxford OX3 8EU
Tel: 0865 66000
Fax: 0865 67676

Badges

London Emblem plc
Emblem House
Blenheim Road
Longmead Industrial Estate
Epsom
Surrey KT19 9AP
Tel: 0372 745433
Fax: 0372 745462

Universal Button Co Ltd
10–12 Witan Street
Bethnal Green
London E2 6JX
Tel: 071 739 5750
Fax: 071 739 1961

Banks

Bank of Scotland
Marketing Department
Uberior House
61 Grassmarket
Edinburgh EH1 2JF
Tel: 0800 838113
Fax: 031 243 5959

Bicycle holders and shelters

George Fischer Sales Ltd
Paradise Way
Coventry CV2 2ST
Tel: 0203 535535
Fax: 0203 530450

Binding equipment

British Printing Industries Federation
11 Bedford Row
London WC1R 4DX
Tel: 071 242 6904
Fax: 071 405 7784

IBICO Ltd
Ibico House
Heston Industrial Estate
Aerodrome Way
Heston
Middlesex TW5 9QB
Tel: 081 759 4833
Fax: 081 564 7901

Boards

Sundeala
Hanworth Road
Sunbury-on-Thames
Middlesex TW16 5DG
Tel: 0932 781749
Fax: 0932 785574

Visible Improvements Ltd
30–34 Brixton Road
London SW9 6DE
Tel: 071 735 4030
Fax: 071 587 0746

Books (suppliers)

Appleby, Myers and Clarke Booksellers
60–64 Market Street
Watford
Hertfordshire WD1 7AR
Tel: 0923 231960
Fax: 0923 246470

Books for Students Ltd
Bird Road
Heathcote
Warwick CV34 6TB

Dillons – The Bookstore
116 New Street
Birmingham B2 4JJ
Tel: 021 631 4333
Fax: 021 643 2408

Jostens School Services
21 Cedar Close
Horsham
Sussex RH12 2BN
Tel: 0403 54264
Fax: 0403 217636

Peters Library Service Ltd
120 Bromsgrove Street
Birmingham B5 6RL
Tel: 021 666 6646
Fax: 021 666 7033

Building

James Longley & Co Ltd
East Park
Crawley
West Sussex RH10 6AP
Tel: 0293 561212
Fax: 0293 564564

Oakmoor Systems
Talewater Works
Talaton
Exeter
Devon EX5 2RT
Tel: 0404 850977
Fax: 0404 850946

Terrapin International Ltd
Bond Avenue
Bletchley
Milton Keynes MK1 1JJ
Tel: 0908 270900
Fax: 0908 270052

Building maintenance

Bushboard Parker Ltd
Rixon Road
Finedon Road Industrial Estate
Wellingborough
Northamptonshire NN8 4BA
Tel: 0933 224983

Willmott Dixon Maintenance
22 Grosvenor Square
London W1X 9LF
Tel: 071 491 9952
Fax: 071 491 7051

Business consultancy

Rank Xerox
Bridge House
Oxford Road
Uxbridge
Middlesex UB8 1HS
Tel: 0895 251133
Fax: 0895 251133 Ext. 3078

Careers

Careers and Occupational Information Centre (COIC)
W1108 Moorfoot
Sheffield S14PQ
Tel: 0742 594564

COIC (Scotland)
247 St John's Road
Edinburgh EH12 7XD
Tel: 031 334 0353

Construction Careers Service
CITB, Bircham Newton
King's Lynn
Norfolk PE31 6RH
Tel: 0553 776677
Fax: 0553 692226

Catering

Britannia Hygiene Ltd
Gibard House
13–15 Dudley Street
Sedgley
West Midlands DY3 1SA
Tel: 0902 678822
Fax: 0902 678558

GLS Fairway Ltd
Ferry Lane
Tottenham Hale
London N17 9NQ
Tel: 081 801 3333

Princes Catering Products
Royal Liver Building
Pier Head
Liverpool L3 1NX
Tel: 051 236 9282

Cleaning

GLS Fairway Ltd
Ferry Lane
Tottenham Hale
London N17 9NQ
Tel: 081 801 3333

Graffiti Clean Ltd
Unit 5, 124A Woodhill
Hillreach
London SE18 5JH
Tel: 081 855 0008
Fax: 081 855 0330

Initial Contract Services
Initial House
81 High Street
Potters Bar
Hertfordshire EN6 5LW
Tel: 0707 4454

Cloakroom facilities

Britannia Hygiene Ltd
Gibard House
13–15 Dudley Street
Sedgley
West Midlands DY3 1SA
Tel: 0902 678822
Fax: 0902 678558

Bushboard Parker Ltd
Rixon Road
Finedon Road Industrial Estate
Wellingborough
Northamptonshire NN8 4BA
Tel: 0933 224983
Fax: 0933 223553

Wessex Hand Driers Ltd
Luscombe Estate
Dawlish
South Devon EX7 0QJ
Tel: 0626 862402
Fax: 0626 888103

Company registration

CFH Company Formations Ltd
58 Redwing
Clanfield
Portsmouth
Hampshire
Tel: 0705 598947
Fax: 0705 596369

Computers, software and systems

ABLAC Computec Ltd
South Devon House
Station Road
Newton Abbot
Devon TQ12 2BP
Tel: 0626 332233
Fax: 0626 331464

Accounting Answers Ltd
Premier Centre
Luzborough Lane
Romsey
Hampshire SO51 9AQ
Tel: 0794 830355
Fax: 0794 830779

Ace Computing
27 Victoria Road
Cambridge CB4 3BW
Tel: 0223 322559

Acorn Computers Ltd
Fulbourn Road
Cherry Hinton
Cambridge CB1 4JN
Tel: 0223 245200
Fax: 0223 210685

Advisory Unit for
Microtechnology in Education
Endymion Road
Hatfield
Hertfordshire AL10 8AU
Tel: 0707 265443
Fax: 0707 273651

Bits and Bytes
21 Commercial Street
Dundee DD1 3DD
Tel: 0382 22052
Fax: 0382 200077

British Aerospace
Space Systems
PO Box 5 Filton
Bristol BS12 7QW
Tel: 0272 693831
Fax: 0272 449452

Campus 2000
TTNS
Priory House
St Johns Lane
London EC1M 4HD
Tel: 071 782 7104
Fax: 071 782 1111

Commodore Business Machines (UK) Ltd
The Switchback
Gardner Road
Maidenhead
Berkshire SL6 7XA
Tel: 0628 770088
Fax: 0628 71456

Dolphin Computer Services Ltd
5 Mercian Close
Watermoor End
Cirencester
Gloucestershire GL7 1LT
Tel: 0285 650960
Fax: 0285 656941

Eltec Computers
2–4 Listerhills Science Park
Campus Road
Bradford BD7 1HR
Tel: 0274 309999
Fax: 0274 731716

GTI Business Systems Ltd
Ashfield Road
Salisbury SP2 7HL
Tel: 0722 338484
Fax: 0722 337167

ICL (UK) Ltd
Studio Way
Borehamwood
Hertfordshire WD6 5QA
Tel: 081 207 6666

Informatic Systems Ltd
ISL House
Lower Park
Park Royal Road
London W3 6XA
Tel: 081 992 9204
Fax: 081 992 5273

Kingsway UK Ltd
73 Northwood Way
Northwood
Middlesex HA6 1RS
Tel: 0923 836473
Fax: 0923 836474

Microsoft
138 Queens Drive
Childwall Fiveways
Liverpool L15 6XX
Tel: 051 722 0304
Fax: 051 737 2127

Nord Education Ltd
South Point
South Accommodation Road
Leeds SL10 1PP
Tel: 0532 444577
Fax: 0532 449420

Packard Bell
Cal Abco House
Braintree Road
Ruislip HA4 0EJ
Tel: 081 842 0071
Fax: 081 841 3891

Rapid Computers Ltd
138 Childwall Fiveways
Liverpool L15 6XX
Tel: 051 722 0304
Fax: 051 737 2127

Research Machines (RM)
Mill Street
Oxford OX2 0BW
Tel: 0865 791234

Rickett Educational Media
Ilton Business Estate
Ilton
Ilminster
Somerset TA19 9HS
Tel: 0460 57151
Fax: 0460 53176

Timetable Systems Ltd
39 Somerset Road
Frome
Somerset BA11 1HD
Tel: 0373 63749

Computer training

Informatic Systems Ltd
ISL House
Lower Park
Park Royal Road
London W3 6XA
Tel: 081 992 9204
Fax: 081 992 5273

Copier control systems

EMOS Information Systems Ltd
Emos House
2 Treadaway Technical Centre
Treadaway Hill
High Wycombe
Buckinghamshire HP10 9RS
Tel: 0628 850400
Fax: 0628 850251

Sarasota Revenue Systems Ltd
King's Worthy
Winchester
Hampshire SO23 7QA
Tel: 0962 883200
Fax: 0962 884026

TDSi Revenue Systems Ltd
Crestworth House
Sterle Avenue West
Poole
Dorset BH15 2AL
Tel: 0202 666222
Fax: 0202 679730

Drama and stage equipment

Donmar Ltd
54 Cavell Street
Whitechapel
London E1 2HP
Tel: 071 790 9937
Fax: 071 790 6634

Stage Systems
PO Box 50
Loughborough
Leicestershire LE11 0GN
Tel: 0509 611021
Fax: 0509 233146

Educational publishers

Cassell
Villiers House
41–47 The Strand
London WC2N 5JE
Tel: 071 839 4900
Fax: 071 839 1809

Paul Chapman Publishing
144 Liverpool Road
London N1 1LA
Tel: 071 609 5315
Fax: 071 700 1057

Collins Educational
HarperCollins
PO Box
Glasgow G4 0NB
Tel: 041 772 3200

HBJ SCHOOLS

RESOURCES FOR EFFECTIVE TEACHING

HBJ Schools offers a wide range of high quality resources for primary and secondary education

PRIMARY   *SECONDARY*

HBJ MATHEMATICS
The complete core programme for Reception to Year 6

LANGUAGE & POWER
An exciting student activities book designed to raise awareness of language

Complete National Curriculum coverage

•

Detailed guidance for teachers

•

Activity-based learning

•

Cost effective materials

INVESTIGATING MINIBEASTS
Flexible materials to help children develop skills in scientific investigation

THE DEVELOPMENT PROJECT
Looks at issues in development in Northern & Southern hemispheres

CATCHWORDS
An effective and popular spelling programme for Key Stages 1 and 2

HOMELESS
A critical approach to homelessness in Britain today for fourth & fifth year students

MULTICULTURAL
Books which raise & discuss issues of concern about today's multicultural society

Send for our latest Primary catalogue now

For more information return the coupon below

HBJ Schools

Please return to:
Harcourt Brace Jovanovich Ltd, **FREEPOST**
Foots Cray High Street, Sidcup, Kent DA14 4BR
Tel: 081 300 3322   Fax: 081 309 0807

Please send me more information about:
☐ HBJ Mathematics
☐ HBJ Schools Primary Resources
☐ HBJ Schools Secondary Resources

Name_____ School _____

Address _____

_____ Post Code _____

SMH0192

299

Falmer Press Ltd
Rankine Road
Basingstoke
Hampshire RG24 0PR
Tel: 0256 840366

HMSO Books
51 Nine Elms Lane
London SW8 5DR
Tel: 071 873 8319
Fax: 071 873 8463

Harcourt Brace Jovanovich Ltd
Foots Cray High Street
Sidcup
Kent DA14 5HT
Tel: 081 300 3322
Fax: 081 309 0807

Hobsons Publishing plc
Bateman Street
Cambridge CB2 1LZ

Hodder and Stoughton
Mill Road
Dunton Green
Sevenoaks
Kent TN13 2YA
Tel: 0732 450111

Kingscourt Publishing Ltd
London House
271–273 King Street
London W6 9LZ
Tel: 081 741 2533
Fax: 081 741 2292

Kogan Page Ltd
120 Pentonville Road
London N1 9JN
Tel: 071 278 0433
Fax: 071 837 6348

Longman Group UK Ltd
6th Floor, Westgate House
The High
Harlow
Essex CM20 1YR
Tel: 0279 442601
Fax: 0279 444501

Thomas Nelson and Sons Ltd
Nelson House
Mayfield Road
Walton-on-Thames
Surrey KT12 5PL
Tel: 0932 246133
Fax: 0932 246109

New Education Press Ltd
13 Church Drive
Keyworth
Nottinghamshire NG12 5FG

Open University Press
Celtic Court
22 Ballmoor
Buckingham MK18 1XW
Tel: 0280 823388
Fax: 0280 823233

Oxford University Press
Walton Street
Oxford OX2 6DP
Tel: 0865 56767
Fax: 0865 56646

Precise Educational
Willowbank House
19 Golden Valley
Riddings
Derbyshire DE55 4ES
Tel: 0773 608722
Fax: 0773 609850

Jonathan Press/Clare Publications
York House
Bacons Lane
Chappel
Colchester CO6 2EB
Tel: 0787 222343

**Publishing and Printing
Services Ltd**
155–157 Oxford Street
London W1R 1TB
Tel: 071 434 0137
Fax: 071 494 1360

Routledge
11 New Fetter Lane
London EC4P 4EE
Tel: 071 583 9855

Energy management

Associated Heat Services plc
2 Salisbury Road
Wimbledon
London SW19 4EZ
Tel: 081 946 2122
Fax: 081 946 1920

CSI World Trade Inc
Building L16
Gyosei International
Business Park
London Road
Reading
Berkshire RG1 5AQ
Tel: 0734 756400
Fax: 0734 750897

**Drayton Controls
(Engineering) Ltd**
Chantry Close
West Drayton
Middlesex UB7 7SP
Tel: 0895 444012
Fax: 0895 421901

**Landis and Gyr
Building Control (UK) Ltd**
2 Dukes Meadow
Millboard Road
Bourne End
Buckinghamshire SL8 5XF
Tel: 0628 850808
Fax: 0626 840797

Environment

Glasdon UK Ltd
The Education Sales Department
Preston New Road
Blackpool
Lancashire FY4 4UL
Tel: 0253 694621
Fax: 0253 792558

Examining bodies

**Business & Technology
Education Council**
Central House
Upper Woburn Place
London WC1H 0HH
Tel: 071 388 3288

City & Guilds of London
46 Britannia Street
London WC1X 9RG
Tel: 071 278 3344
Fax: 071 278 9460

Joint Council for the GCSE
8th Floor, Netherton House
23–29 Marsh Street
Bristol BS1 4BP
Tel: 0272 214379

Midland Examining Group
Norfolk House
Smallbrook Queensway
Birmingham B5 4NJ
Tel: 021 631 2151

Northern Examining Association
c/o The Joint Matriculation Board
Manchester M15 6EU
Tel: 061 273 2565

**Northern Ireland Schools
Examinations Council**
Beechill House
42 Beechill Road
Belfast BT8 4RS
Tel: 0232 704666

**Oxford and Cambridge Schools
Examination Board**
Elsfield Way
Oxford OX2 8EP
Tel: 0865 54421
and
Purbeck House
Purbeck Road
Cambridge CB2 2PU
Tel: 0223 411211

RSA Examinations Board
Westwood Way
Coventry CV4 8HS
Tel: 0203 470033
Fax: 0203 468080

Scottish Examination Board
Ironmills Road
Dalkeith
Midlothian EH22 1LE

The Southern Examining Board
Central Administration Office
Stag Hill House
Guildford
Surrey GU2 5XJ
Tel: 0483 503123

**University of London
Examinations and
Assessment Board**
The Lindens
Lexden Road
Colchester C03 3RL
Tel: 0206 549595

Welsh Joint Education Committee
245 Western Avenue
Cardiff CF5 2YX
Tel: 0222 561231

Excursions and talks

The Ackers Trust
Golden Hillock
Small Heath
Birmingham B11 2PY
Tel: 021 771 4448

The Arc
Archaeological Resource Centre
St Saviourgate
York
Tel: 0904 643211
Fax: 0904 627097

Cadbury World
PO Box 1958
Linden Road
Bournville
Birmingham B30 2LD
Tel: 021 459 9116
Fax: 021 451 1366

The Duke of Edinburgh's Award
Gulliver House
Madeira Walk
Windsor
Berkshire SL4 1EU
Tel: 0753 810753
Fax: 0753 810666

The Expedition Advisory Centre
1 Kensington Gore
London SW7 2AR
Tel: 071 581 2057

Gower Tours Ltd
2 High Street
Studeley
Warwickshire B80 7HJ
Tel: 052785 4822
Fax: 052785 7236

Jorvik Viking Centre
Coppergate
York YO1 1NT
Tel: 0904 643211
Fax: 0904 640028

Northumberland Activity Holidays
Northumberland Business Centre
Southgate
Morpeth
Northumberland NE61 2EH
Tel: 0670 511221
Fax: 0670 510878

Outward Bound Trust
Chestnut Field
Regent Place
Rugby CV21 2PJ
Tel: 0788 560423

Parliamentary Education Unit
Room 507
Norman Shaw Building (South)
Victoria Embankment
London SW1A 2HZ
Tel: 071 219 4750
Fax: 071 219 5839

The Prevention of Alcohol and Drug Misuse and Abuse
Clouds House
East Knoyle
Salisbury SP3 6BE
Tel: 0747 830733
Fax: 0747 830783

Space School
Brunel University
Uxbridge
Middlesex UB8 3PH
Tel: 0895 71490
Fax: 0895 746608

Tambrands Ltd
Dunsbury Way
Havant
Hampshire PO9 5DG
Tel: 0705 474141
Fax: 0705 451110

Wales Tourist Board
Brunel House
2 Fitzalan Road
Cardiff CF2 1UY
Tel: 0222 499909
Fax: 0222 485031

Exhibitions display/design

ATLAS Exhibitions International
Hanborough Business Park
Lodge Road
Hanborough
Oxford OX7 2LH
Tel: 0993 883434

Marler Haley Exposystems Ltd
Beaconsfield Close
Hatfield
Hertfordshire AL10 8XB
Tel: 0707 268155
Fax: 0707 276677

RAL Display and Marketing Ltd
Midlands Display Showroom
2 Cranmer Street
Leicester LE3 0QA
Tel: 0533 554640
Fax: 0533 550572

SD Systems Ltd
Unit 2, Cressex Business Complex
Lancaster Road
High Wycombe
Buckinghamshire HP12 3PY
Tel: 0494 465212
Fax: 0494 465145

Sundeala Board Company Ltd
Sundeala House
Hanworth Road
Sunbury-on-Thames
Middlesex TW16 5DG
Tel: 0932 781749
Fax: 0932 785574

Financial advice

Buro Four Project Services
296–300 St John Street
London EC1V 4PP
Tel: 071 833 8663
Fax: 071 833 8560

Coopers and Lybrand Deloitte
Chartered Accountants
PO Box 207
128 Queen Victoria Street
London EC4P 4JX
Tel: 071 583 5000
Fax: 071 248 3623

MacIntyre & Co
Chartered Accountants
28 Ely Place
London EC1N 6RL
Tel: 071 242 0242
Fax: 071 495 4786

Floor coverings

Altro Floors
Works Road
Letchworth
Hertfordshire SG6 1NW
Tel: 0462 480480
Fax: 0462 480010

Heckmondwike F B Ltd
PO Box 7
Wellington Mills
Liversedge
West Yorkshire WF15 7XA
Tel: 0924 406161
Fax: 0924 409972

London Artid Plastics/Duragrid
Falmouth Road
Slough SL1 4SE
Tel: 0735 27661
Fax: 0753 692334

Nuway Manufacturing Co Ltd
Halesfield 19
Telford
Shropshire TF7 4QT
Tel: 0952 680400
Fax: 0952 585930

St Annes Contract Carpeting (Bristol) Ltd
1 Repton Road
Sandy Park
Brislington
Bristol BS4 3LS
Tel: 0272 774804
Fax: 0272 771000

Tufton Ltd
21 East Parade
Harrogate
North Yorkshire HG1 5LF
Tel: 0423 530001
Fax: 0423 501645

Fundraising

CR Consultants
6 Coldbath Square
London EC1R 5HL
Tel: 071 833 0414
Fax: 071 833 0188

Peeks of Bournemouth Ltd
Riverside Lane
Tuckton
Bournemouth BH6 3LD
Tel: 0202 417777

'Schoolgoal'
Haydock High School
Clipsley Lane
Haydock
St Helens
Merseyside WA11 0JG
Tel: 0744 54221

Webb Ivory
Primrose Hill
Preston PR1 4EL
Tel: 0772 822212
Fax: 0772 830102

Furniture suppliers

British Telecom
PO Box 3
Wythenshawe
Manchester M22 4SS
Tel: 061 998 1311
Fax: 061 946 0242

Budget Direct Ltd
Global House
38–40 High Street
West Wickham
Kent BR4 0NE
Tel: 081 777 0099

Castelli (UK) Ltd
316–318 Regent Street
London W1R 5AB
Tel: 071 323 3320
Fax: 071 323 5635

eibe-play ltd
5 Trevor Avenue
Sale
Cheshire M33 4DJ
Tel: 061 962 8295

Ercol Furniture Ltd
London Road
High Wycombe
Buckinghamshire HP13 7AE
Tel: 0494 21261
Fax: 0494 462467

GLS Fairway Ltd
Ferry Lane
Tottenham Hale
London N17 9QN
Tel: 081 801 3333

For further information please contact:-

WILL BECK LIMITED

Kitchener Chair Works
Kitchener Road
High Wycombe,
Buckinghamshire HP11 2SW
Telephone: (0494) 524466
Facsimile: (0494) 526835

Registered with the British Standards Institute and manufactured to the highest standards, including ignition source 5. All timber is beech but available stained natural, light oak, teak or mahogany. Any fabric available including Ambia vinyls and Cambourne Mainline FR – ask for catalogues and switches.

QUALITY   ASSURANCE

B.S. 5750 part 2
Cert. No. FM 13338

T551/FWH

The Premier chair for the elderly with good support. Supplied with either vinyl or soft cover with any or all of depicted extras, i.e. wings, filled in sides, armpads, handgrips. Seat height 17"-21". Matching stool available.

STRENGTH AND QUALITY AT AFFORDABLE PRICES

T504
Comfortable low armchair with or without arms (T506) available with high back or as a 2 or 3 seater.

The Buckingham
A small, large or circular occasional table. Also dining tables available.

T548
With 17" seat height. A comfortable stylish armchair with or without arms (T547) and available as a 2 or 3 seater.

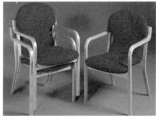

ALL
BRITISH
DESIGNED
AND
BUILT

Piccadilly Armchair
A new stacking armchair from the Henley Collection. Ask for a full catalogue.

Piccadilly Sidechair
A new stacking sidechair from the Henley Collection. Ask for full catalogue.

Gopak Ltd
Range Road
Hythe
Kent CT21 6HG
Tel: 0303 265751
Fax: 0303 268282

Hayes and Finch Ltd
Hanson Road
Aintree
Liverpool L9 7BP
Tel: 051 523 6303
Fax: 051 525 1246

Hope Education
Orb Mill
Huddersfield Road
Waterhead
Oldham OL4 2ST
Tel: 061 633 6611
Fax: 061 633 3431

Hille Polypropylene Products Ltd
Tafarnaubach Industrial Estate
Unit 26, Tredegar
Gwent NP2 3AA

Hostess Furniture
Vulcan Road
Bilston
West Midlands WV14 7JR
Tel: 0902 493681

Papworth Group
Papworth Everard
Cambridge CB3 8RG
Tel: 0480 830345
Fax: 0480 830781

Pel plc
Oldbury
Warley
West Midlands B69 4HN
Tel: 021 552 3377
Fax: 021 552 6067

Portastor (High Security Cabinets)
Portasilo Ltd
Freepost
York YO1 1US
Tel: 0904 624872

P&L Products Ltd
Edisto House
Peartree Industrial Estate
Upper Langford
Bristol BS18 7DJ
Tel: 0934 853222
Fax: 0934 853218

Remploy Ltd
Remploy Profile
Lakeside Technology Park
Phoenix Way
Enterprise Park
Swansea SA7 9FL
Tel: 0792 775400
Fax: 0792 775611

Rhondeau Ltd
(Steel Cabinets and Lockers)
Unit 4
George Bayliss Road
Berry Hill Industrial Estate
Droitwich
Worcestershire WR9 9AB
Tel: 0905 773300

Sherwood Industries
Southwell Road West
Rainworth
Mansfield
Nottinghamshire NG21 0HW
Tel: 0623 792151
Fax: 0623 796530

Unicol Engineering
Green Road
Headington
Oxford OX3 8EU
Tel: 0865 66000
Fax: 0865 67676

VS Furniture
Hochhauser Strasse 8
PO Box 1420
D-6972 Tauberhischofscheim
Germany
Tel: 010 49 93 41 880
Fax: 010 49 93 41 8810

Will Beck Ltd
Kitchener Chair Works
Kitchener Road
High Wycombe
Buckinghamshire HP11 2SW
Tel: 0494 24466
Fax: 0494 26835

Wilson and Garden Ltd (Boards)
17–21 Newtown Street
Kilsyth
Glasgow G65 0JX
Tel: 0236 823291
Fax: 0236 825683

Grants

The Centre for the Study of Comprehensive Schools (CSCS)
The Queens Building
University of Leicester
Barrack Road
Northampton NN2 6AF
Tel: 0604 24969

Health and safety

GLS Fairway Ltd
Ferry Lane
Tottenham Hale
London N17 9QN
Tel: 081 801 3333

The Royal Society for the Prevention of Accidents
Cannon House
The Priory Queensway
Birmingham B4 6BS
Tel: 021 200 2461
Fax: 021 200 1254

Insurance

Frizell Education Insurance
Bolton House
56–58 Parkstone Road
Poole
Dorset BH15 2PH
Tel: 0202 765050
Fax: 0202 684428

Holmwoods Ltd
Rockwood House
9–17 Perrymount Road
Haywards Heath
West Sussex RH16 1TA
Tel: 0444 458144
Fax: 0444 415088

IT specialists

Coopers and Lybrand Deloitte Chartered Accountants
PO Box 207
128 Queen Victoria Street
London EC4P 4JX
Tel: 071 583 5000
Fax: 071 248 3623

MacIntyre & Co
Chartered Accountants
28 Ely Place
London EC1N 6RL
Tel: 071 242 0242
Fax: 071 405 4786

The Times Network Systems
(TTNS)
Priory House
St Johns Lane
London EC1M 4HD
Tel: 071 782 7104
Fax: 071 782 7111

Laboratory equipment

Ecomonatics (Education) Ltd
Epic House
Darnall Road
Attercliffe
Sheffield S9 5AA
Tel: 0742 561122
Fax: 0742 439306

Griffin and George
Bishopmeadow Road
Loughborough
Leicestershire LE11 0RG
Tel: 0509 233344

Marlec Engineering Co Ltd
Unit K
Cavendish Courtyard
Sallow Road
Corby
Northamptonshire NN17 1DZ
Tel: 0536 201588
Fax: 0536 400211

Pyser Ltd
Fircroft Way
Edenbridge
Kent TN8 6HA
Tel: 0732 864111
Fax: 0732 865544

Laminating

IBICO Ltd
Ibico House
Heston Industrial Estate
Aerodrome Way
Heston
Middlesex TW5 9QB
Tel: 081 759 4833
Fax: 081 564 7901

Morane
5 Haslemere Way
Banbury
Oxfordshire OX16 8TT
Tel: 0295 67927
Fax: 0295 51109

Library equipment

Book Protectors & Co
Department CRX
Protector House
76 South Grove
London E17 7NJ
Tel: 081 520 0012

Don Gresswell Ltd
Bridge House
Grange Park
London N21 1RB
Tel: 081 360 6622
Fax: 081 360 9231

LFC (Library Furnishing Consultants)
Denington Road
Wellingborough
Northamptonshire NN8 2RF
Tel: 0933 422777
Fax: 0933 442764

Library Resources Exhibition
2 Forge House
Summerleys Road
Princes Risborough
Buckinghamshire HP17 9DT
Tel: 0844 42894
Fax: 0844 44988

Remploy Lundia
Lundia Centre
Ashton Road
Oldham
Lancashire OL8 3JG
Tel: 061 626 4119
Fax: 061 627 0313

B Serota Ltd
Acme Works
Rendlesham Road
Clapton
London E5 8PS
Tel: 081 985 1736
Fax: 081 985 5109

Terrapin Interiors
Bond Avenue
Bletchley
Milton Keynes MK1 1JJ
Tel: 0908 270900
Fax: 0908 270052

VS Furniture
Hochhauser Strasse 8
PO Box 1420
D-6972 Tauberhischofsheim
Germany
Tel: 010 49 93 41 880
Fax: 010 49 93 41 88230

Lighting

GE Thorn Lamps Ltd
Miles Road
Mitcham
Surrey CR4 3RX
Tel: 081 640 1221
Fax: 081 685 9625

Management consultants

Buro Four Project Services
296–300 St John Street
London EC1V 4PP
Tel: 071 833 8663
Fax: 071 833 8560

Coopers and Lybrand Deloitte Chartered Accountants
PO Box 207
128 Queen Victoria Street
London EC4P 4JX
Tel: 071 583 5000
Fax: 071 248 3623

Neville Russell
246 Bishopgate
London EC2M 4PB
Tel: 071 377 1000
Fax: 071 377 8931

Marketing

Keith Bates Associates
9 Ingestre Road
Hall Green
Birmingham B28 9EQ
Tel: 021 777 6050

Express Gifts
Church Bridge House
Henry Street
Accrington
Lancashire BB5 4EE
Tel: 0254 382121
Fax: 0254 383693

Music

Educational Aids (London) Ltd
George Street
Irthlingborough
Northamptonshire NN9 5RH
Tel: 0933 650970

eibe-play ltd
5 Trevor Avenue
Sale
Cheshire M33 4DJ
Tel: 061 962 8295

GLS Fairway Ltd
Ferry Lane
Tottenham Hale
London N17 9QN
Tel: 081 801 3333

Orcarina Workshop
PO Box 56
Kettering
Northamptonshire NN15 6RH
Tel: 0536 85963

Schott
48 Great Marlborough Street
London W1V 2BN
Tel: 071 437 0263

Stewart Orr Sound Services
Prior's Croft Barn
Withersdale
Harleston
Norfolk IP20 0JG

Office equipment

Office — copiers

Abingdon Photocopying
38 Swinbourne Road
Abingdon
Oxfordshire
Tel: 0235 527972

Emos Information Systems Ltd
Emos House
2 Treadaway Technical Centre
Treadaway Hill
High Wycombe
Buckinghamshire HP10 9RS
Tel: 0628 85040
Fax: 0628 850251

Canon (UK) Ltd
1 Peall Road
Croydon
Surrey CR0 3EX

Dataproducts Ltd
Unit 1 Heron Industrial Estate
Spencers Wood
Reading
Berkshire RG7 1PJ
Tel: 0734 884777
Fax: 0734 88345

CONTROL YOUR COPYING COSTS

Photocopying is one of the most useful reprographic facilities in schools, colleges and libraries, but to accurately monitor its use and cost, a Copier Control System is a great advantage.

POST ACCOUNTING

Copymanager CM10 is attached to the copier. This micro-processor control unit has a memory holding up to 1500 accounts. Authorised users access the unit by keying in a Personal Identification Number (PIN) up to six digits or by swiping a magnetic plastic card with their account number. At the end of the month the system supervisor accesses the unit with a menu card and can read off account totals. Alternatively a portable printer can be connected and a printout obtained showing account and group totals. The unit has the facility to assign group (department) numbers to individual accounts.

PRE ACCOUNTING

The Copytex CX3000 terminal is attached to the copier. It only accepts Value Cards which are sold or issued to authorised users. Value cards have a magnetic stripe encoded with a unique client system number and a number of copy units – rather like a phone card. The system supervisor specifies the values to be encoded on the cards by EMOS. For instance, a school could have £1 cards encoded with say, 15 copies to be sold to students and other cards encoded with any appropriate number eg; 500 or 1000 copies to be issued to staff. With the CX3000 it is possible to charge differentially for A3 and A4 copies.

THE CASE FOR CONTROL AND CASHLESS SYSTEMS

- Enables you to exercise **BUDGETARY CONTROL** over an important discretionary spend.

- **UNIVERSAL** copier control system as EMOS units fit all makes and model of copier.

- Can **REDUCE COPY VOLUME** by up to 20% – saves costs and saves paper.

- **TOTAL COPIER SECURITY** – only authorised users can use the copier.

- 100% **ACCOUNTING** for all copies made.

- **CASHLESS** – Card Systems.

  - Less cash handling

  - School obtains cash "up front"; improves cash flow.

  - Easier administration

EMOS
INFORMATION SYSTEMS LTD

EMOS House, 2 Treadaway Technical Centre, Treadaway Hill, High Wycombe, Bucks HP10 9RS
Telephone: (0628) 850400 Facsimile: (0628) 850251

Kodak Ltd
PO Box 66
Station Road
Hemel Hempstead
Hertfordshire HP1 1JU

Rank Xerox
Bridge House
Oxford Road
Uxbridge
Middlesex UB8 1HS
Tel: 0895 251133
Fax: 0895 251133 Ext. 3078

Office furniture

Bushboard Parker Ltd
Rixon Road
Finedon Road Industrial Estate
Wellingborough
Northamptonshire NN8 4BA
Tel: 0933 224983
Fax: 0933 223553

Castelli (UK) Ltd
316–318 Regent Street
London W1R 5AB
Tel: 071 323 3320
Fax: 071 323 5635

Portastor High Security Products
Portasilo Ltd
Freepost
York YO1 1US
Tel: 0904 624872

VS Furniture
Hochhauser Strasse 8
PO Box 1420
D-6972 Tauberhischofsheim
Germany
Tel: 010 49 93 41 880
Fax: 010 49 93 41 88230

Office — general

Erskine Ltd
Head Office
Erskine House
Oak Hill Road
Seven Oaks
Kent TN13 1NW
Tel: 0732 460044
Fax: 0732 451179

GLS Fairway Ltd
Ferry Lane
Tottenham Hale
London N17 9NQ
Tel: 081 801 3333

Don Gresswell Ltd
Bridge House
Grange Park
London N21 1RB
Tel: 081 360 6622
Fax: 081 360 9231

Informatic Systems Ltd
ISL House
Lower Park
Park Royal Road
London W3 6XA
Tel: 081 992 9204
Fax: 081 992 5273

Rank Xerox
Bridge House
Oxford Road
Uxbridge
Middlesex UB8 1HS
Tel: 0895 251133
Fax: 0895 251133 Ext. 3078

Total Mailroom Systems
St John's House
Carrigill
Alston
Cumbria
Tel: 0434 381182
Fax: 0434 382035

Office supplies and stationery

Berol Ltd
Oldmedow Road
King's Lynn
Norfolk PE30 4JR
Tel: 0553 761221
Fax: 0553 766534

Birmingham City Supplies Organisation
25 Pollman Street
Nechells
Birmingham B7 4RT
Tel: 021 333 3030
Fax: 021 333 3180

GLS Fairway Ltd
Ferry Lane
Tottenham Hale
London N17 9NQ
Tel: 081 801 3333

Don Gresswell Ltd
Bridge House
Grange Park
London N21 1RB
Tel: 081 360 6622
Fax: 081 360 9231

Kroy (Europe) Ltd
Worton Grange
Reading
Berkshire RG2 0LZ
Tel: 0734 861411
Fax: 0734 863451

QSS Ltd
Mill House
11 Nightingale Road
Horsham
West Sussex RH12 2NW
Tel: 0403 65511
Fax: 0403 69726

NES Arnold Ltd
Ludlow Hill Road
West Bridgford
Nottingham NG2 6HD
Tel: 0602 452200

Rank Xerox
Bridge House
Oxford Road
Uxbridge
Middlesex UB8 1HS
Tel: 0895 251133
Fax: 0895 251133 Ext. 3078

Staedtler (UK) Ltd
Pontyclun
Mid Glamorgan CF7 8YJ
Tel: 0443 237421
Fax: 0443 237440

Paint suppliers

Johnstone's Paints
Stonebridge House
Droylsdon
Manchester M35 6BX
Tel: 061 370 7525
Fax: 061 370 8318

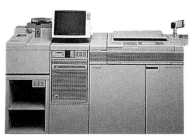

316

Physical education and sport

Amateur Swimming Association
Harold Fern House
Derby Square
Loughborough
Leicestershire LE11 0AL
Tel: 0509 230431
Fax: 0509 610720

Educational Aids (London) Ltd
George Street
Irthlingborough
Northamptonshire NN9 5RH
Tel: 0933 650970

eibe-play ltd
5 Trevor Avenue
Sale
Cheshire M33 4DJ
Tel: 061 962 8295

GLS Fairway Ltd
Ferry Lane
Tottenham Hale
London N17 9QN
Tel: 081 801 3333

Sutcliffe Leisure Ltd
Sandbeds Trading Estate
Dewsbury Road
Ossett
West Yorkshire WF5 9ND
Tel: 0924 280028
Fax: 0924 276155

Play equipment

Community Playthings
Robertsbridge
East Sussex TN32 5DR
Tel: 0580 880626
Fax: 0580 881171

eibe-play ltd
5 Trevor Avenue
Sale
Cheshire M33 4DJ
Tel: 061 962 8295

Hope Education
Orb Mill
Huddersfield Road
Waterhead
Oldham OL4 2ST
Tel: 061 633 6611
Fax: 061 633 3431

Nevawood Ltd
Unit 3
Snibston Drive
Ravenstone Road
Coalville
Leicester LE6 2NB
Tel: 0530 511049
Fax: 0530 530961

WESCO
15 Avenue de la Gare
BP 37
F 79140 Cerizay
France
Tel: 010 33 49 80 0166
Fax: 010 33 49 80 0333

Photographic

GLS Fairway Ltd
Ferry Lane
Tottenham Hale
London N17 9QN
Tel: 081 801 3333

H Tempest Ltd
The Colour Laboratory
St Ives
Cornwall TR26 3UH
Tel: 0736 752411
Fax: 0736 754851

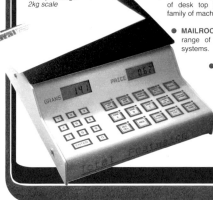
318

Professional bodies

Association of Accounting Technicians
154 Clerkenwell Road
London EC1R 5AD
Tel: 071 837 8600
Fax: 071 837 6970

Independent Association of Preparatory Schools
11 Waterloo Place
Leamington Spa
Warwickshire CV32 5LA
Tel: 0926 887833

Institute of Financial Accountants
Burford House
44 London Road
Sevenoaks
Kent TN13 1AS
Tel: 0732 458080
Fax: 0732 458568

Institute of Training and Development
Marlow House
Institute Road
Marlow
Buckinghamshire SL7 1BD
Tel: 0628 890123
Fax: 0628 890208

The Library Association
7 Ridgmount Street
London WC1E 7AE
Tel: 071 636 7543
Fax: 071 436 7218

Publications

Educational Management and Administration
CEMPS
School of Education
University of Birmingham
PO Box 63
Birmingham B15 2TT

Education Equipment
58 Fleet Street
London EC4Y 1JU

Education Guardian
The Guardian
119 Farringdon Road
London EC1R 3ER
Tel: 071 278 2332
Fax: 071 837 1267

Education Today
Datateam Publishing Ltd
Datateam House
Tovil Hill
Maidstone
Kent ME15 6QS
Tel: 0622 687031
Fax: 0622 757646

Head Teachers' Review
1 Heath Square
Boltro Road
Haywards Heath
West Sussex RH16 1BL

Headlines
Hobsons Publishing plc
Bateman Street
Cambridge CB2 1LZ

Management in Education
Harcourt Brace Jovanovich Ltd
Foots Cray High Street
Sidcup
Kent
Tel: 081 300 3322
Fax: 081 309 0807

Managing Schools Today
The Questions Publishing
Company Ltd
6–7 Hockley Hill
Hockley
Birmingham B18 5AA
Tel: 021 507 0850
Fax: 021 554 7513

Times Educational Supplement
Priory House
St John's Lane
London EC1M 4BX
Tel: 071 253 5000
Fax: 071 251 4698

Recruitment

Coopers and Lybrand Deloitte
Chartered Accountants
PO Box 207
128 Queen Victoria Street
London EC4P 4JX
Tel: 071 583 5000
Fax: 071 248 3623

Teacher Recruitment Project:
Manchester City Council
Education Department
Education Officer
Crown Square
Manchester M60 3BB
Tel: 061 234 7175
Fax: 061 234 7073

VSO
317 Putney Bridge Road
London SW15 2PN
Tel: 081 780 2266
Fax: 081 780 1326

School bells

CIC Systems of Cambridge Ltd
119 Mill Road
Cambridge CB1 2AZ
Tel: 0223 312346
Fax: 0223 323257

School fees

Schoolplan
(John P McDonald & Associates
t/a)
Office No 7
The Commercial Business Centre
Kendricks Cross
Rainhill
Merseyside L35 4LP
Tel: 051 430 8061
Fax: 051 430 7836

Security

Security — Access control

Ambassador Security Group plc
Hermitage Court
Hermitage Lane
Barming
Maidstone
Kent ME16 9NT
Tel: 0622 720780
Fax: 0622 720646

**CSI Control Systems
International**
Building L16
Gyosei International Business
Park
London Road
Reading
Berkshire RG1 5AQ
Tel: 0734 756400
Fax: 0734 750897

Cash and Security Equipment Ltd
Security House
Acrewood Way
St Albans
Hertfordshire AL4 0JL
Tel: 0727 868203
Fax: 0727 41079

Feedback Data Ltd
Bell Lane
Uckfield
East Sussex TN22 1PT
Tel: 0825 761411
Fax: 0825 768238

Thomas Laidlaw Security
Sterling House
South Shore Road
Gateshead
Tyne and Wear NE8 3AE
Tel: 091 477 4433
Fax: 091 477 1014

NBS Ltd
Unit 7, Canada Road
Byfleet Industrial Estate
Byfleet
Surrey KT14 7JL
Tel: 0932 351531
Fax: 0932 351382

TDSi Revenue Systems Ltd
Crestworth House
Sterle Avenue West
Poole
Dorset BH15 2AL
Tel: 0202 666222
Fax: 0202 679730

Security — Alarms

Ambassador Security Group plc
Hermitage Court
Hermitage Lane
Barming
Maidstone
Kent ME16 9NT
Tel: 0622 720780
Fax: 0622 720646

Alarmcom Ltd
Baddow Park
West Hanningfield Road
Great Baddow
Chelmsford
Essex CM2 7SY
Tel: 0245 478585
Fax: 0245 478530

**CSI Control Systems
International**
CSI World Trade Incorporated
Building L16
Gyosei International Business
Park
London Road
Reading RG1 5AQ
Tel: 0734 756400
Fax: 0734 750897

Cash and Security Equipment Ltd
Security House
Acrewood Way
St Albans
Hertfordshire AL4 0JL
Tel: 0727 868203
Fax: 0727 41079

Datatech Wiring
3 West Burrowfield
Welwyn Garden City
Hertfordshire AL7 4TW
Tel: 0707 339137
Fax: 0707 320148

Security — Bar code technology

Feedback Data Ltd
Bell Lane
Uckfield
East Sussex TN22 1PT
Tel: 0825 761411
Fax: 0825 768238

Markitwise International
Homme Castle Farm
Sheisley Walsh
Worcestershire WR6 6RR
Tel: 0886 5427
Fax: 0886 5243

Security — Closed-circuit TV

Ambassador Security Group plc
Hermitage Court
Hermitage Lane
Barming
Maidstone
Kent ME16 9NY
Tel: 0622 720780
Fax: 0622 720646

Cam Era Holdings
Kembury House
5 Worcester Road
Bromsgrove B61 7DL
Tel: 0527 579669
Fax: 0527 579739

Cash and Security Equipment Ltd
Security House
Acrewood Way
St Albans
Hertfordshire AL4 0JL
Tel: 0727 868203
Fax: 0727 41079

Security — Library security systems

3M UK PLC
3M House
1–6 PO Box 1
The Marketplace
Bracknell
Berkshire RG12 1JU
Tel: 0344 858162
Fax: 0344 858479

Security — Locks

Camlock Systems Ltd
2 Park View
Compton Industrial Estate
Eastbourne BM23 6QE
Tel: 0323 410996
Fax: 0323 411512

Thomas Laidlaw Security
Sterling House
South Shore Road
Gateshead
Tyne and Wear NE8 3AE
Tel: 091 477 4433
Fax: 091 477 1014

Security — Marking

Markitwise International
Homme Castle Farm
Sheisley Walsh
Worcestershire WR6 6RR
Tel: 0886 5427
Fax: 0886 5243

Selecta Security Systems Ltd
The Gatehouse
5 Locks Court
429 Crofton Road
Locksbottom
Kent BR6 8NL
Tel: 0698 860757
Fax: 0689 860693

Security — Passive infra-red

Alarmcom Ltd
Baddow Park
West Hanningfield Road
Great Baddow
Chelmsford
Essex CM2 7SY
Tel: 0245 478585
Fax: 0245 478530

Cam Era Holdings
Kembury House
5 Worcester Road
Bromsgrove B61 7DL
Tel: 0527 579669
Fax: 0527 579739

Setsquare
5A Valley Industries
Hadlow Road
Tonbridge
Kent TN11 0AH
Tel: 0732 851888
Fax: 0732 851853

Security — Photographic surveillance

Cam Era Holdings
Kembury House
5 Worcester Road
Bromsgrove B61 7DL
Tel: 0527 579669
Fax: 0527 579739

Cash and Security Equipment Ltd
Security House
Acrewood Way
St Albans
Hertfordshire AL4 0JL
Tel: 0727 868203
Fax: 0727 41079

Solicitors

Wedlake Saint Solicitors
14 John Street
London WC1N 2EB
Tel: 071 405 9446
Fax: 071 242 9877

Special educational needs

Dyslexia Institute
133 Gresham Road
Staines
Middlesex TW18 2AJ
Tel: 0784 463851
Fax: 0784 460747

eibe-play ltd
5 Trevor Avenue
Sale
Cheshire M33 4DJ
Tel: 061 962 8295

Gifted Children's Information Centre
Hampton Grange
21 Hampton Lane
Solihull B91 2QJ
Tel: 021 705 4547

Learning Development Aids
Duke Street
Wisbech
Cambridgeshire PE13 2AE
Tel: 0945 63441

PLANET (Play Leisure Advice Network)
c/o Harperbury Hospital
Harper Lane
Shenley
Nr Radlett WD7 9HQ
Tel: 0932 854861

Teaching materials

The Bible Society
Stonehill Green
Westlea
Swindon SN5 7DG
Tel: 0793 513713
Fax: 0793 512539

Christian Aid
PO Box 100
London SE1 7RT
Tel: 071 620 4444
Fax: 071 620 0719

Duke of Edinburgh's Award
Gulliver House
Madeira Walk
Windsor
Berkshire SL4 1EU
Tel: 0753 810753
Fax: 0753 810666

Electricity Education Services
30 Millbank
London SW1P 4RD
Tel: 071 834 2333
Fax: 071 233 6640

Geopacks
Michael Jay Publications
PO Box 23
St Just
Penzance
Cornwall TR19 7JS
Tel: 0736 787808
Fax: 0736 787880

Health Education Authority
Hamilton House
Mabledon Place
London WC1H 9TX
Tel: 071 383 3833
Fax: 071 387 0550

Hope Education
Orb Mill
Huddersfield Road
Waterhead
Oldham OL4 2ST
Tel: 061 633 6611
Fax: 061 633 3431

Lancashire Education Resources Unit
PO Box 61 County Hall
Fishergate
Preston PR1 8RJ
Tel: 0772 263771
Fax: 0772 263630

Marketing Matters Ltd
Orchard House
Marshes End
Poole Road
Poole
Dorset BH17 7AG
Tel: 0202 673846
Fax: 0202 679326

Montessori Equipment Co Ltd
18 Balderton Street
London W1Y 1TG
Tel: 071 493 0165
Fax: 071 629 7808

Precise Educational
Willowbank House
19 Golden Valley
Riddings
Derbyshire DE55 4ES
Tel: 0773 608722
Fax: 0773 609850

RSPCA
Causeway
Horsham
West Sussex RH12 1HG
Tel: 0403 64181
Fax: 0403 41048

Save the Children Education Unit
17 Grove Lane
London SE5 8RD
Tel: 071 703 5400
Fax: 071 703 2278

UK Atomic Energy Authority
Education Officer
Building 354 West
AERE Harwell
Didcot
Oxfordshire OX11 0RA
Tel/Fax: 0235 821111

Teachers' unions

Assistant Masters' and Mistresses' Association (AMMA)
7 Northumberland Street
London WC2N 5OA
Tel: 071 930 6441

National Association of Head Teachers
1 Heath Square
Boltro Road
Haywards Heath
West Sussex RH16 1BL
Tel: 0444 458133
Fax: 0444 416326

NASUWT
Hillscourt Education Centre
Rednal
Birmingham B45 8RS
Tel: 021 453 6150
Fax: 021 453 7224

National Union of Teachers (NUT)
Hamilton House
Mabledon Place
London WC1H 9BD
Tel: 071 388 6191

The Professional Association of Teachers
2 St James Court
Friar Gate
Derby DE1 1BT
Tel: 0332 372337
Fax: 0332 290310

Television

MacCulloch and Wallis Ltd
25–26 Dering Street
London W1R 0BH
Tel: 071 629 0311
Fax: 071 491 2481

Thorn EMI Business Communication
Highfield House
Foundation Park
8 Roxborough Way
Maidenhead
Berkshire SL6 3TZ
Tel: 0628 822181
Fax: 0628 822865

Time and attendance registration

NBS Ltd
Unit 7, Canada Road
Byfleet Industrial Estate
Byfleet
Surrey KT14 7JL
Tel: 0932 351351
Fax: 0932 351382

Training and information

Action for Governors
Information and Training
AGIT, Community Education
Development Centre
Lyng Hall
Blackberry Lane
Coventry CV2 3JS
Tel: 0203 638660
Fax: 0203 681161

Birmingham Lea Governor
Training and Support Unit
Education Office
Margaret Street
Birmingham B3 3BU
Tel: 021 235 2322

The Centre for School Effectiveness
Westminster College
North Hinksey
Oxford OX2 9AT
Tel: 0865 245242

Centre for the Study of Comprehensive Schools
The Queens Building
University of Leicester
Barrack Road
Northampton NN2 6AF
Tel: 0604 24969
Fax: 0604 36326

The College of Preceptors
Coppice Row
Theydon Bois
Epping
Essex CM16 7DN
Tel: 0992 812727
Fax: 0992 814690

Dyslexia Institute
133 Gresham Road
Staines
Middlesex TW18 2AJ
Tel: 0784 463851
Fax: 0784 460747

Economic Awareness Teacher Training Programme (EcATT)
University of Manchester
School of Education
Oxford Road
Manchester M13 9PL
Tel: 061 273 4452

Institute of Training and Development
Marlow House
Institute Road
Marlow
Buckinghamshire SL7 1BD
Tel: 0628 890123
Fax: 0628 890208

Montessori St Nicolas Centre
23–24 Princes Gate
Knightsbridge
London SW7 1PT
Tel: 071 225 1277
Fax: 071 823 7557

National Association of Governors and Managers
26 Laystall Street
London EC1R 4PQ
Tel: 071 833 0399

National Association of Head Teachers
1 Heath Square
Boltro Road
Haywards Heath
West Sussex RH16 1BL
Tel: 0444 458133
Fax: 0444 416326

The National Primary Centre
Westminster College
North Hinksey
Oxford OX2 9AT
Tel: 0865 245242

The ORT Trust
ORT Resource Centre
Queen Mary and Westfield College
Kidderpore Avenue
London NW3 7ST
Tel: 071 794 0029
Fax: 071 431 4598

Roehampton Institute
School of Education
Froebel College
Roehampton Institute
Roehampton Lane
London SW15 5PJ

The School of Education
University of Birmingham
Edgbaston
Birmingham B15 2TT
Tel/Fax: 021 414 4865

Secondary Heads' Association (MAPS)
130 Regent Road
Leicester LE1 7PG
Tel: 0533 471797

Teacher Placement Service – UBI
Sun Alliance House
New Inn Hall Street
Oxford OX1 2QE
Tel: 0865 722585

Transport

Autosave
Lydgate House
Lydgate Lane
Sheffield S10 5FH
Tel: 0742 667166
Fax: 0742 684269

Kirkham Minibuses
Blackpool Road
Kirkham
Preston
Lancashire PR4 2RE
Tel: 0772 684922
Fax: 0772 671162

Red Kite Ltd
3 Haddons Drive
Three Legged Cross
Wimbourne
Dorset BH21 6QU
Tel: 0202 827678
Fax: 0202 827029

Skills Bus Ltd
35 Floribunda Drive
Briar Hill
Northampton NN4 9RZ
Tel: 0604 764394

Vending machines

Coca-Cola and Schweppes Beverages Ltd
Corporation Street
Corby NN17 1NG

Concept Vending International
Unit 18
Looner Road Industrial Estate
Newcastle under Lyme
Staffordshire ST5 7LB
Tel: 0782 566070
Fax: 0782 564603

Vendustrial Ltd
Great North Road
Graveley
Hitchin
Hertfordshire SG4 7EQ
Tel: 0462 672011
Fax: 0462 482795

Video

CTVC
The Foundation for
Christian Communication Ltd
Hillside Studios
Merry Hill Road
Bushey
Watford WD2 1DR
Tel: 081 950 4426
Fax: 081 950 1437

Focus in Education
Video Training Packages
Duke Street
Wisbech
Cambridgeshire PE13 2AE
Tel: 0945 63441

Thorn EMI Business Communications
Highfield House
Foundation Park
8 Roxborough Way
Maidenhead
Berkshire SL6 3TZ
Tel: 0628 822181
Fax: 0628 822865

Water management

Britannia Hygiene Ltd
Gibard House
13–15 Dudley Street
Sedgley
West Midlands DY3 1SA
Tel: 0902 678822
Fax: 0902 678558

Bushboard Parker Ltd
Rixen Road
Finedon Road Industrial Estate
Wellingborough
Northamptonshire NN8 4BA
Tel: 0933 224983
Fax: 0933 223553

Setsquare Ltd
5A Valley Industries
Hadlow Road
Tonbridge
Kent TN11 0AH
Tel: 0732 851888
Fax: 0732 851853

Waste management

United Kingdom Nirex Ltd
Curie Avenue
Harwell
Didcot
Oxfordshire OX11 0RH
Tel: 0235 835153
Fax: 0235 831239

Workwear and protective clothing

GLS Fairway Ltd
Ferry Lane
Tottenham Hale
London N17 9NQ
Tel: 081 801 3333

Index of Advertisers

Abingdon Photocopying, 4
Accounting Answers Ltd, 47
Alarmcom Ltd, 172
Ambassador Security Group plc, 193
Associated Heat Services plc, 152
Association of Accounting Technicians, 199
Bank of Scotland, 5
Bits and Bytes, 247
Books for Students Ltd, 66
Bovis Construction Ltd, 230
Britannia Hygiene plc, 225
James Burn International, 84
Buro Four Project Services, 241
BushBoard Parker Ltd, 142
Cam Era Holdings Ltd, 196
Camlock Systems, 172
Campus 2000, 256
CASE Cash and Security Equipment Ltd, 174
Castelli UK Ltd, 65
CFH Company Formations Ltd, 296
Concept Vending International Ltd, 270
Coopers and Lybrand Deloitte, 61
CSI Control Systems International, 186
CTVC Video, 198
Dataproducts Ltd, 216
Datatech Wiring, 174
Drayton Controls (Engineering) Ltd, 160
EcATT Programme, 86
eibe-play Ltd, **144**
Electricity Association, 212
EMOS Information Systems Ltd, 312
Ercol Furniture Ltd, 72

Erskine Ltd, 314

Express Gifts, 118

Feedback Data Ltd, 187 and 264

Flexicard TDSi, 266

Focus in Education, 103

Frizell Education Insurance, 53

GE Thorn Lamps Ltd, 167

GLS Fairway Ltd, 76

Gopak Ltd, 98

Graffiti Clean Ltd, 144–145

Don Gresswell Ltd, 192

Griffin and George, 93

The Guardian, 95

Harcourt Brace Jovanovich Ltd, 299

Heckmondwike F B Ltd, 110

Holmwoods Ltd, 56

Hope Education Ltd, 106

Ibico Ltd, 132

Informatic Systems Ltd, 316

Initial Contract Services, 222

Intac Data Systems Ltd, 254

Johnstone's Paints, 122

Kingsway UK Ltd, 251

Thomas Laidlaw Security, 184

Landis and Gyr Building Control Ltd, 154

Library Copy Services Ltd, 116

London Electricity, 156

James Longley and Co Ltd, 149

MacCulloch and Wallis Ltd, 218

MacIntyre and Co, 42

Markitwise International, 176

Mars Electronics International, 130

Micromail Data Supplies, 247

Morane Ltd, 188

National Rejectors Inc, 268

Nat West Bank plc, 14–15

NBS Ltd, 178

NCET Publications, 204

Nuway Manufacturing Co Ltd, 204

Osram Ltd, 166

P and L Products, 208

Papworth Group, 208

Portable Buildings Ltd, 232

Portakabin Ltd, 229

Potterycrafts Ltd, 261
Princes Catering Products, 200
Production Engineering Ltd, 187
The PSA, 234–235
Rank Xerox, inside front cover and 214
Rhondeau Ltd, 276
Rickitt Educational Media, 278
Satchwell Control Systems, 162
Selectamark Security Systems Ltd, 182
Setsquare, 168
Shepherd Building Group, 173
Shorrock Ltd, 176
Smith Kline Beecham, 114
Solutions Ltd, 7
Telecom Security, 180–181
THE Solutions Ltd, 249
Thorn EMI Business Communications, 100
3M (United Kingdom) plc, 190
Times Educational Supplement, 37
Total Mailroom System Ltd, 318
United Kingdom Nirex Ltd, 6
VS Furniture, 290
Wedlake Saint, 35
Will Beck Ltd, 306
Willmott Dixon Maintenance Ltd, 232